CW00589906

Who Am I Without M~~y~~ ......

Written
By

Rebecca Bishop

Art by HERAKUT

Jasmin Siddiqui
&
Falk Lehmann

ISBN: 9781092852845

Dedication

This book is dedicated to Hollie Gazzard, and all other women who have lost their lives at the hands of their abuser. Hollie symbolises the reasons why we owe it to victims to understand the impacts of Psychological abuse.

To all women who have been abused and sieved like

sand,

may you read this book and find grains of yourself,

in places that you never thought to look!

Contents

Don't you worry, said the mermaid, for as long as you can see me,

they have not yet stolen your freedom

About the Author

My name is Rebecca; In 2006 I was in an extremely abusive relationship. You see things on TV that document how toxic a person can be, but you never truly understand monsters until you meet one. I was living in a real-life nightmare that replayed cycles of anger, upset and apologies. People often tell victims who leave their abuser 'your safe, your free'. In reality healing from an abusive relationship is long, messy and not a straight line. The voice that stays with you after the abuse is his and that voice is something you have to fight to get rid of long after you leave. Recovering from abuse can make you feel insane, it's like seeing a lightning bolt but hearing his voice telling you that there is no storm. I know what is real, but sometimes I still catch my eyes cursing themselves for their perfect vision.

On Leaving my abusive relationship I wanted to understand domestic abuse on every possible level I could and then with this knowledge I pledged to help as many other people as I could. I have studied the psychology of humans for over 10 years and have gained two degrees, one in Social Sciences and one in Counselling. I began working with victims of domestic abuse in 2012 and started teaching the professionals that support them about the impact of domestic abuse in 2017. I have worked with hundreds of victims that have been affected by the impacts of domestic abuse. Through this experience I have recognised that everyone has their own story of abuse, but there are many similarities that we all share. Humans are all the same on basic biological levels, we can all be controlled, manipulated and brainwashed. I began to see patterns in how we become victims of abuse, which is why I have decided to share my ideas. I write in the hopes that the cycle of abuse that others experience can be recognised, understood and stopped.

For me this cycle was like a hamster wheel; everything was moving so fast there was no time to think. I forgot who I was, and the wheel just kept turning. I never questioned when he said it was my fault; I always believed him when he said I was the chaos.

So many victims I work with do not like the word victim but you still have more control than you know. You may have been a victim of abuse, but you still have power over your own self. You may feel that this power has been taken from you by your abuser, but you can take this back if you believe you can. I believed that my abuser took my inner and outer beauty! He didn't take my beauty, he took my confidence, but for a while I didn't realize they were the same thing! I have written this book for you, for you to find your confidence here, because for me, this book did not exist when I needed it. This book is full of connections that I have made over the last 12 years, I hope that some of it speaks to you. I share with you my findings and my ideas of freedom, but how you get there is on your own.

How to use this book

This book can be used by anyone who would like to understand the impact of abuse on female victims from male perpetrators. Victims, professionals and others alike will gain more knowledge about victim and perpetrator need's and behaviours.

If you are a victim: you'll need a notepad to do each task that you come across when reading through. The book is filled with ideas about what makes you a person and ideas about how to feel better after abuse.

If you are a family member or friend: read the book to understand the reasons and the impacts of domestic abuse. Although this book is primarily for women who have been victim to domestic abuse, it can be read by others who would like to understand abusers and victims.

If you are a professional supporting a victim: use this book to understand the impact of abuse. You can carry out the tasks in this book with the victim to help them work towards overcoming their issues. The book can be used in the form of a workshop in groups, or on an individual basis.

Introduction

Hey you! You may be here because you have experienced something that has changed your life! Something that not many other people understand, something that you should never have had to understand. Or maybe you are a professional or loved one of a victim and wish to support them in understanding their experiences. While men are also affected by abuse, this book is for women who have experienced abuse. The reason that this book does not cover same sex abuse or women perpetrators is because the ways in which abuse happens in these relationships can be slightly different than male to female abuse. The book is written in this way as my experience and knowledge is mainly with female victims and male perpetrators. Throughout this book we look at separating the body and mind, and to try and understand abuse, its impacts and how to move forward.

For the women who are here because of their experiences, I wrote this book to take each one of you on a journey through who you were, who you are now, and who you can be. The book encourages you to use your own ideas to search every corner of your being, so that you can make sense of your experience. From reading this book you will gain insight in to the following:

- Understanding what types of abuse, you experienced

- Know the cycles of abuse and how they continue

- Understand your needs and why you have them

- Understand how your past may have shaped you

- Know the common symptoms that others experience

- Understand your emotions

- Connect your experiences with your current mental health

- See how society shapes our ideas on abuse

- Look at your experience as a human issue not just an individual one

- Know what healthy emotions are

- Know different coping skills to deal with the impacts of abuse

I have worked as a counsellor with people who suffer from addictions, disorders and mental health issues, all of which are recognised as having a hold over the person they affect. Yet domestic abuse is looked upon as something you can easily overcome … that the moment you gain freedom you can happily start to piece your life back together … that it's something to celebrate.

I have too often heard the question: why didn't they just leave? This book looks at the reasons why you stay and the truth about being free. Being out of the relationship does not mean that you are happy or free; unpicking all the scrambled parts of your brain will take time. Freedom can be scary, and it can take a while to get there. It's OK to miss your relationship, it's OK to say that you miss being controlled – having control again can be frightening.

When I became 'free' I couldn't decide if I wanted a straw or not with my drink let alone make any meaningful life decisions. I want to send the message that it's OK to not know how to live life in your own shoes for a while, it's OK to say that you still feel attached and connected to your ex-partner. Its also safe to still feel scared, if this concern is real then you may find the help available in the back pages of this book can help.

This book recognises you as a human as well as your individual life experience. It allows you to unpick your past and personality. It allows you to understand your reasons for staying in an abusive relationship and how to get to know yourself even better than before! We start by looking at what domestic abuse is, then follow on to popular ideas about what type of person can become a victim or a perpetrator. This popular idea stems through the professional world and although there is a definite cycle of abuse, we now need to acknowledge that there is so much more at play! Not all victims of abuse are from broken homes, or vulnerable positions. Some are from amazing homes with no vulnerabilities and they still become victims of abuse. We need to acknowledge the dynamics of abusive relationships and how they can break even the strongest person.

We look at other issues such as the many victims that are given multi diagnosis following their experience of abuse, because these symptoms are all usually the result of their abuse. I liken abusers to interrogators of war, we look at war tactics and their effects on prisoners in comparison to domestic abuse tactics and its impacts. Using ideas about multi diagnosis and the impacts of war tactics, I propose that the impacts of abuse should be looked at as not 2, or 3, but one mental health issue. I carried out a study with over 50 women who have experienced domestic abuse. The main findings showed that women experience the same symptoms following an abusive relationship. I want to encourage people from all walks of life to recognise these symptoms and understand that abuse changes your brain in a way that shapes your entire being. You develop all sorts of issues as a result of abuse and I have termed these collective symptoms as *Attachment Capture Syndrome*.

This book in its entirety tries to cover as many different issues as possible, some of the topics covered may not be relevant to you as an individual. However domestic abuse is so complex I felt it necessary to give insight in to the many issues that arise from it. You will find self-help tasks scattered through the book to help you understand yourself and to learn to start living again. The book concludes with many different techniques that I have used to support victims of abuse. I share with you my ideas on abuse to encourage you to make sense of your own journey or to understand someone else's.

Chapter 1

The complexities of domestic abuse- what is really going

on?

Now I am almost ready for your kind of love

We often categorise types of domestic abuse, there is one underlying type of abuse that underpins all abuse, this is known as 'coercive control'. Coercive control enables an abuser to carry out any type abuse because while it is present, the victim will accept the way they are treated. This chapter starts by looking at the complexities in each type of abuse as well as examples of what this type of abuse is.

Psychological Abuse

Most victims that have experienced both psychological and physical abuse have said that the psychological abuse was for them, worse than the physical abuse. After experiencing psychological abuse, I have seen victims that have so little confidence in their ability, that they can't even make a phone call. Your psychological wellbeing seems to have two main parts, which are: how you view yourself and how you perceive how others see you. I believe that psychological abuse is any type of abuse that effects the way you see yourself or the way you think others see you. Both views interact with the other, if someone says you are unable, you might question yourself with: 'am I able if this person thinks I am not?'

Below is an example of psychological abuse:

You are about to make a phone call to pay a bill you owe; your partner is watching you call. While you are making the call your partner sniggers, laughs and shakes his head. When the call is over, your partner says, 'they must have thought you were an idiot, the way you were going on.'

Being judged in this way would make you begin to question yourself; you start to pick apart every sentence you say to others. And after the interaction is over, you can't help but think how others viewed you. You might be good at many different things, you might be a good cook, a good communicator or have good dress sense. But receiving continuous criticisms about what you do wrong can make you feel like it is all wrong or not good enough. For many people the idea of this happening is strange; there is little to no understanding of how this could happen. But this type of behaviour is more common than you think and can be seen in all walks of life. People with power over you can dominate the way that you view yourself. I give an example here:

A well-known body builder who was admired by many, would train alongside his opponents with the intention of causing self-doubt. He would question his opponent's choice of weightlifting and methods of exercises. 'You're not lifting that like that, are you?' he would gasp at his opponents. His opponents started to change the weights they lifted and the ways in which they lifted them. They started to question whether they were making the best choices and then changed their methods. With these changes and the stress of being judged, the body builder's opponents deteriorate in the weeks that lead up to the competition.

Here the body builder takes advantage of his gained reputation and used this to control how others view themselves. This type of psychological manipulation was done with no use of threats but rather through the reputation of being superior. This shows that psychological abuse can be carried out without threatening behaviour if the person creates the idea that they are superior in some way.

Most people can be brainwashed into thinking negatively about themselves and what they do. However, some negative views are easier to accept than others. I'd say we all carry with us reactions that we would have had from our childhood experiences. For instance:

You were 'always' told 'don't be silly' when you were growing up, yet now as an adult you recognise you are not as stupid as you were once told. You get involved with a perpetrator who knows you used to be called stupid, because of this he keeps reaffirming that you are silly or stupid. You then change your own belief system about yourself and begin to believe that you are stupid. This belief may be easy to accept because he confirms what others have already said.

Most people want to share their past and upbringing with their new partner, and in many circumstances, this information will not be used negatively to exploit your trust. However, when you share this information with a perpetrator, they will then know the views and experiences that you had that you find negative. You may have told him certain things that people have said about you that really hurt you. So, here you have given him the things that upset you and now he knows what negative views about yourself that you will easily believe. From working as, a counsellor, I have noted that most clients can connect their current belief system with their childhood experiences. I know as a child I believed everything my parents, friends or teachers told me, because these were the people that mattered to me. I often explore with clients the fact that their abuser would say things that they knew would affect them most. An abuser takes all of the insecurities that they know you have from your childhood and magnifies them. Victims have reported that due to this explosion of childhood insecurities, they feel more childlike in the sense that they start to feel more vulnerable and unconfident. I would suggest that by default, this seems to make you more dependent on the abuser. This dependency feeling again mirrors how you felt about adults as a child.

In fact, I have recognised that the perpetrator assumes the adult role and the victim becomes the vulnerable child; They are easily dominated by him and view their abuser as superior. This pattern is shown in the cycle below.

Cycle from confident adult to inner child

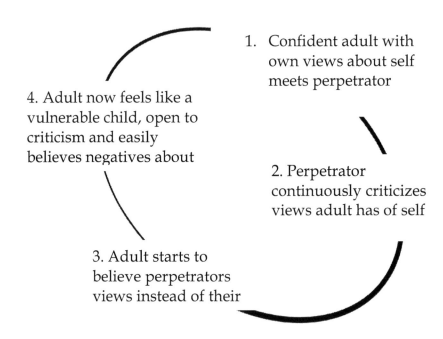

4. Adult now feels like a vulnerable child, open to criticism and easily believes negatives about

1. Confident adult with own views about self meets perpetrator

2. Perpetrator continuously criticizes views adult has of self

3. Adult starts to believe perpetrators views instead of their

When you are operating from this vulnerable child position you truly believe most negative beliefs that you now hold about yourself. When victims have assumed this role, it seems that they will accept any negative views about themselves, even negative views that are not connected to their childhood. When I have viewed victims that are in this vulnerable place, they tend to have doubt in anything that they do and find it difficult to feel any sort of independence or confidence. These negative thought patterns remain long after the abusive relationship ends and can take a long time to change.

Perpetrators who know how to use psychological abuse may carry out abuse in a more sinister way. Abusers have played purposeful tricks on victims – they have moved keys, coats, toothbrushes and many other household things. Following this they suggest that you have lost them just to make you feel like you are losing your mind. They may even present you with the item, and, in this scenario, they are the hero and you are inept. Victims have reported that this type of abuse makes you feel like you are losing your sanity. This can change your views on yourself to the point that you no longer trust your own judgment. You start to feel like you are lucky to have someone in your life who is so stable to help you, and this makes you see them as superior. This enables them to carry out psychological abuse on you even easier because you value their opinions more than your own. This form abuse is now known as Gaslighting.

Emotional abuse

I recognise emotional wellbeing as two-parts: how you feel your feelings and how you express those feelings. I have noted that emotional abuse is any type of abuse that is carried out to evoke negative emotions or abuse that stops you from expressing your emotions. Here is an example of both:

Your partner said horrible things in anger; it made you extremely upset. So, upset that you began to cry. When you began to cry your partner got angrier. He shouted at you for crying, accusing you of being a drama queen and trying to make him feel bad. You immediately stopped crying.

In this example, upset was not allowed; crying was not allowed so you could not express your sadness. This type of abuse can also be when you are not allowed to be angry or even judged for being too happy. You learn to hide your emotions and are unsure of how to express your feelings. You suppress your actions and over time you are not able to manage your feelings. I often hear victims say that it is this type of abuse that can make them feel numb.

I have asked victims how they feel and many often reply with: I don't know.' I conclude that when we must supress our emotions for a long time, we can lose touch with how we feel. This can lead to negative coping mechanisms, because our emotions still need to be expressed in some way. Negative coping can include drugs, drinking, eating disorders, self-harm, mental health issues, risky behaviours and negative thoughts. I feel that suppressing feelings can make you less able to understand your feelings and as your conscious mind tries to push them away, your unconscious mind will be storing them inside somewhere! This means that even though you feel numb and are unaware of your feelings, they will be trying to surface in some form or another.

Emotions are strange, and you can never really know how others feel. You can only imagine what they might feel from the words they tell you. There may have been times during your own abusive relationship where you say the words 'I love you', in order to avoid a conflict. Many women say that when they were being verbally or even physically attacked, they have said 'I love you' in the hopes it will make their abuser stop. When you are in this position you will say 'I love you' with conviction to make it as meaningful as possible. But do you really mean it in this position?

What do you love about this person, now, in this moment, as they are being abusive towards you? We have all heard the stories in the media about people who get kidnapped and held hostage for years. For the few people that have escaped from this situation there is a sense of freedom. But surprisingly they sometimes say that they loved their captor. Some even view that they were in a relationship with them despite having been kidnapped and held against their will.

The fact that survivors of abductions say that they love their captors is fascinating to say the least. Just like victims of domestic abuse, kidnapped people express love and kindness towards their abuser. They do this to avoid potential harm and with the intention to survive. They know in these situations that being loving and showing kindness will make their captor happy. This example suggests that if we act this way with conviction for long periods of time, we may start to believe it. So, after a while, pretending to feel something is essentially making you feel something for real. This can be confusing when the underlying reason that we convey love, is fear. I suggest that this is not real love, it is a survival technique that we use to avoid harm, unfortunately we can do it so well, we believe it ourselves. Your need to survive takes over your mind and emotions, your expressions of love feel real and a strong bond is formed between you and your abuser. Can you think back to a time you might have said I love you to stop negative situations? Did you really feel love at this point?

Physical Abuse

I feel that physical abuse effects every part of your wellbeing. Physical abuse is touch abuse; it's contact to the skin. This is where I have noticed differences in how the abuse makes some women feel. Physical abuse seems to change the way your body wants to react. It is difficult to see the body and mind as separate entities, but this is what they are. If you imagine that these two parts of you are disconnected it is easier to see how symptoms of physical and sexual abuse affect you differently to other types of abuse. After experiencing physical abuse many women disclose that their body has develop triggers or reactions that do not make any sense.

See the following example which shows how this might happen:

Following the ending of a physically abusive relationship, a woman experiences fears that her neck will break. In any situation that may cause injury she immediately panics about her neck. One day she fell of her bike and feared that she had broken her neck, despite the fall being minor. She also fears when anyone touches around her collar bone and has a kneejerk reaction to pull backwards. This woman became ill with a sore throat and started having panic attacks because she thought that she could not breathe. The panic attacks disturb her ability to breathe, which then makes it even more real that she can't breathe.

All these issues are separate issues that happened; this woman did not know that they were all connected. This woman was strangled on many different occasions; she has put this to the back of her mind and continues to live her life. Her body, however, was reminding her in many different situations that what happened was unsafe. A lot of women have triggers that make them panic or relive memories. This woman developed a reflex reaction where she pulled backwards when somebody touched anywhere near her neck. We found that this reaction was connected to being nervous of harm to the neck area. Her body had experienced so much physical pain that it now reacts quickly, without her even knowing why.

Some incidents of physical abuse can sometimes be so severe it damages the way your body works in the future. This type of physical injury is difficult to overcome as it may have changed elements of your life forever. I have heard victims that have had life changing injuries say that learning to use their body again gave them a different identity. And this surprisingly made them happy because they celebrated the success of feeling strength in learning how to use their body again.

Physical abuse can emphasise the emotional and psychological fears you have about leaving your abuser. If they have hurt you before then this is your proof that they can hurt you again; knowing this will make future threats more believable. If you do genuinely believe that your ex-partner could harm you, there are safety measures that are highlighted in the back on this book.

Many victims say that they don't know how they felt when they were being physically attacked, they just lived it and went through it at the time with no thoughts about it. I propose that this is because physical abuse can happen so fast that you do not have any time to process what is happening. What I mean by this is that victims suggest that when they have been physically hurt, their abuser will quickly make them feel like it's their fault. This can be by telling them things like, 'look how angry you have made me' or cry about how upset they are at what they have done. I feel that this furthers your inability to process what has happened; instead you forget about the abuse and you concentrate on how your abuser feels.

Sexual abuse

Sexual abuse can be any form of sexual behaviour that is unwanted, or that you do not want to be part of or that you are too young to consent to. Here we look at sexual abuse that happens in adult relationships rather than child sexual abuse. Some forms of sexual abuse are easier to recognise than others; if you do not consent to the sexual behaviour then this is abuse. But what about if you don't want to but do not say no? In the not-so-distant past, it was not considered rape if you were married, it was a 'wife's duty'. The unfortunate thing about these old views is, that they still filter down through generations. In these views some perpetrators do not see that it is sexual abuse because it is something that is expected, and others will just use these views to get what they want. If you live with these views being thrown at you for long enough, they become your norm, and saying no just does not seem appropriate. But you have the right to say no; if you feel it is your duty or that you must do it rather than want to, this is sexual abuse.

Not many people recognise that sexual abuse can also be when your partner withholds sex. Maybe they are punishing you and have withdrawn all intimacy, maybe they are telling you they can't sleep with you because they don't find you attractive. This form of abuse can make you feel worthless; this form of abuse also sends you the message that you are not attractive. It is not difficult to see in this scenario that you would feel like you would never be able to get a new partner because you are not attractive to others. This by default has made some victims want to stay with their partner even more – you feel lucky when they are attentive and hope that they don't leave.

Following sexual abuse, it can be very difficult to accept affection from others. Sexual abuse is mostly skin-to-skin contact. Almost all victims I have worked who have been sexually abused have said that they find it hard to receive hugs off loved ones and can not bare to be touched by others. You may want to push people away when they comfort you. After some victims have experienced sexual abuse, they have said they feel that they are not worthy of others affection. Others have said that they do not like themselves enough to receive loving affection. Before learning how to be OK with yourself, you must first know what it is that's wrong. Knowing your triggers and what your bodily reactions are connected to will eventually make it easier to understand how to move forward. Knowing this will make everything less confusing. You can begin to relate what is happening to a reason rather than feel you have no idea.

Coercive control

Coercive control is not one act of control but rather ongoing controlling behaviours to have power over another. Coercive control is present in most abusive relationships. Without coercive control it is unlikely that any other type of abuse can exist. For someone to become an abuser they must have some level of control over their victim or they can not carry out their abuse. Some of the examples below fit into the categories of emotional, psychological, physical and sexual abuse. However coercive control is the underpinning of abuse and consists of the following behaviour:

- Intimidating/threatening

- Demands

- High expectancies of you

- Belittling, both in public and alone

- Ignoring your needs

- Punishing for not following demands
- Harm against pets

- Isolating you from others

- Causing arguments between you and others

- Controlling all finances

- Not wanting you to work

- Controlling food intake and clothing

- Using drugs to control

- Forcing pregnancy or abortion

- Manipulation

- Promises

- Lies

Control can be exerted vindictively as some perpetrators seek out women with children or disabilities to claim access to higher rates of benefits. This kind of perpetrator has pre-planned their actions, and they actively look for people that will be easy to control. This type of abuser can use elements of control that are not even recognised by some victims. This pattern has been seen in prisoners of war that were captured and tortured. Over time the prisoners said that they adapted their behaviour based on their captor's ideas. They tried to show similarities between their captors and themselves and took on all their thoughts and views. Eventually there may be little distinction between what thoughts are yours and what are theirs. (Biderman, 1957; Farber et al, 1957) We look in more depth at this notion in a later chapter, but first we continue to look at controlling behaviours.

Some abused women are told not to wear certain clothes because they look fat, easy or ugly. These insults might come from a place of jealousy and insecurity that others may be attracted to you. The abusers need to control how others view you can be achieved with controlling how you dress. On leaving abusive relationships many women I have worked with still choose not to wear certain clothes as they believe that they look fat, easy or ugly. They can not tell their own mind from their abusers, and only see what their abuser said.

Coercive control can be even more confusing when control has also been present in your social life. Your abuser may have criticised your friends and family to the point where you believed the same things he did about them. This would make you distrust others, hold negative views for others and make you less likely to want to socialise. Alternatively, he may start an argument every time you chose to visit a family member or friend because of the ideas he has about them. This in turn would have made you more isolated and more dependent on your abuser.

The following types of abuse are also coercive control. However, these types can be used specifically to distort your reality:

- Minimisation: Perpetrators may minimise what they have done to you so that you start to believe what they have done is OK

- Claims you are deluded: They may cheat on you but when confronted start accusing you of being paranoid, deluded or jealous

- Denial: They may deny their actions if you confront them about why they have mistreated you

- Excuses: They may make excuses that involve their past experiences their addictions or life struggles. This can sometimes involve crying to gain sympathy

- Blaming you or others: They may also blame others for your relationship troubles: 'it's because your sister doesn't like me'; 'your friends lead you astray'; 'your mother hates me'

Controlling perpetrators may try to break relationships you have, making you argue with others. This type of abuser may also decide to make those relationships better again, saying: 'I'll talk to them for you'; 'I'll get them to be OK with you again'. This again is a way of playing the hero that you need. All the above controlling behaviours make you question yourself and your reality, which falls under the term highlighted earlier as Gas lighting.

Controlling behaviour can even be masked as nice behaviours which can therefore go undetected for a long time. This could be that they say, 'aww, why are you leaving me to go out with your friends, I will miss you too much.' If this is what someone says every time you want to go out, this could be considered coercive control.

Controlling behaviour does not have to be aggressive or physical. Intimidating behaviour can sometimes be enough to make you believe that violence will follow. An example of this type of behaviour is:

Your partner has made you think they are going to hit you by flinching their whole body towards you. However, they retreat and do not touch you.

This gesture provokes fear and it is your imagination of what could have happened that can leave you worried about what he could do in the future. This is a severe example, but threatening control can also involve an aggressive stare, a verbal threat, raising their hand or telling you stories of abuse they have done in the past.

Blackmail is another common controlling abusive behaviour that may make you want to stay with the abuser. If the perpetrator holds information that could cause you conflict, they may threaten to tell other people about it if you leave. They may hold information about you that professionals would disapprove of and threaten to disclose this information if you leave. In these cases, it is so important to know that trained domestic abuse workers are aware of this type of blackmail. Things like this that are shown to a worker by an abuser would highlight that they are abusive. I have worked with women that have chosen to stay for many years because their abuser possessed videos of them acting inappropriately. They feared that they would show them to their family. Other women have been forced to stay with their partner out of fear that they may lose their life. We look now at the threats that can follow an abusive relationship that ends.

Is this stalking?

Many people that have a relationship that comes to an end would not view their ex-partner as a stalker. It may sound crazy, but many people think that a stalker is unknown and secretly sends you things. But this is not often the case, a stalker can be an ex-partner who calls you ten times a day to ask you to get back together. Maybe at this point you can think of an ex who has just tried to hold on longer than you would have liked. We can often confuse the fact that this is stalking since we know the person. Stalking can be sending gifts, reems of text messages, phone calls, turning up where you are or contacting friends and family members of yours.

However, stalking can also be where they bad mouth you to others or threaten to commit suicide. If an ex-partner is persistent in their stalking behaviours it is important to seek help with this situation. This book is dedicated to Hollie Gazzard who was abused by her ex-partner. Hollie was coercively controlled by her partner and when she chose to leave her relationship her partner was not willing to let Hollie go. Her ex-partner continuously called her and threatened her and her family. Hollie's ex-partner turned up at the hair salon where she worked and stabbed her 14 times, killing her. Hollies farther Nick Gazzard has been working to help victims of abuse to be safer from their abusers. Nick highlights that there are domestic abuse support services in every county. The *Hollie Guard* has been developed following the murder of Hollie, this is an app that can be downloaded to smart phones. This app has several different features on it, one of which allows you to save a chosen contact to your phone and in the event of a crisis, shaking your phone will immediately alert your chosen person with your location. With this app you can also set a journey that you are about to walk and send it to your contact, the phone will track you via GPS and will alert your contact if you have stopped or when you are safe. This app has been recommended by several police forces and I know that this app will save lives! The dangers of stalking and threatening behaviour following the end of an abusive relationship are serious. Although you know this person and do not think they would harm you, the truth is they might. If an abuser threatens you or your loved ones, you must take this seriously. Stalking is sometimes looked at by others as empty threats, however Hollies death shows that any threats that abuser makes must not be ignored. If you feel that you are unsupported in your reports to police or support services, choose an alternative support. There are other services and advice available in the back of this book that will be able to provide you further support.

Do not attempt to manage a stalker by yourself, there are people that can help.

Looking at the above ideas of what domestic abuse is, it is easy to recognise that abuse does affect a person's being in many complex ways. I tell most abuse victims that how they feel following their abuse is almost a normal feeling, a normal reaction to what they have experienced. A lot of victims can not see how they deteriorated, and they therefore do not recognise that what they currently feel is a result of their abuse.

How did I deteriorate?

I view that your mental health is kind of in three parts: your psychological wellbeing; your emotional wellbeing; and your social wellbeing. As noted above I feel that: your psychological wellbeing is how you view yourself and how you perceive that others view you. Your emotional wellbeing is how you feel your feelings and how you express these feelings. Your social wellbeing is how you make and maintains relationships. I have noticed that for many people if any of these areas are affected in a negative way, it can contribute to a deterioration of mental health. People in an abusive relationship will often develop or have exacerbated mental health issues.

The table below shows all three parts of your mental health. There is a X in the boxes that will be affected by each type of abuse:

ABUSE	PSYCHOLOGICAL	EMOTIONAL	SOCIAL

	WELLBEING	WELLBEING	WELLBEING
Psychological	X	X	X
Emotional	X	X	X
Physical	X	X	X
Sexual abuse	X	X	X
Coercive control	X	X	X

Looking at this table shows that it is inevitable that metal health is going to be affected by domestic abuse. We all should recognise that mental health is paper-thin; we all fluctuate from time to time with how we cope. Taking into consideration the above types of abuse it seems completely normal that you are not going to be OK. It is normal to be anxious; it is normal to feel lost, disconnected, unconfident and low. It is OK that you are not OK: look at what you have been through and note that this may not be you, but rather behaviours you have picked up from reacting to abuse. We look at how you deteriorate in more depth in Chapter 3, but first we look at other possible dynamics that could exist in an abusive relationship.

Chapter 2

Is love really the answer?

If love is the answer could you please rephrase the

question?

The Language of love

Linguistics has a lot to answer for! And by this, I mean language, the words we use – how we communicate, and how we translate what we're hearing. Words can evoke pain, love, laughter and anger. We put so much meaning on the words people say; words are our tool and we can use them to build someone up or knock them down. So many times, abuse victims have been convinced by the words that have been said to them. Many victims believe that their partner fiercely loved them, loved them too much to bear.

Words have been used to make them feel unique, words like 'you're not like other girls; there's something different about you'. What does that even mean? Of course, you're different you're the only one of you. These words imply that you are special, there has been 'no one' like you before. Words like this send you the message that you are the most meaningful person to someone, and you believe these words when they are said to you.

Abusers sometimes say things that are powerful, like: 'I could never live without you'. These words tell you that you are so meaningful, that life would be unbearable without you. Do these extreme words hold any meaning at all, or are they said to make you believe that you are important? If they are said with any meaning, they could be even more alarming. If you could not live without someone doesn't that show that your happiness is dependent on them – that you rely on them to make you happy … if they are gone you cannot be happy. This is such a big responsibility; how can you always maintain being someone's happy, and should you really be expected to be? You should never be someone's happy because this means you will also be their sad. Words can sometimes have hidden meanings; words allow us to tell others that we are a certain type of person. The age old saying 'actions speak louder than words' hold truth when it comes to ideas of love, we return to this idea later in the book but first we look at how words can be used to knock you down.

Just when you are on top of the world and feel that you have met the love of your life, words can change that. Conflicting words are thrown at you: 'I never wanted to be with you'. The shock of hearing these words at first leaves you in disbelief, they leave you confused and unsure of your worth to this person. How can you go from the best thing in their life to the worst thing?

The idea that feelings can be withdrawn so quick gives uncertainty to your sense of worth. This leaves you in a state of confusion, in a position where it is difficult to trust the words people say. Of course, there are things that people can do which immediately change your feelings but for an abuser these may be small things that should not be considered as bad. Perpetrators use words as a tool, the language of love is easy if you know how to use it. Victims believe that what they had was love, but perpetrators often know what you want to hear, and they use this to make you feel secure. Only when you feel secure do they then have the power to use words that break you down.

We too easily believe words that are said with conviction, we want to feel loved so much that when we hear kind words, we want to believe them. Actions are overlooked by the words that we want to hear. When you are shown actions that do not fit words, it is the actions that hold the truth. It can be extremely difficult to accept that the person you were with did not love you. After all they did say that you were *the one*. If a person can say I love you and withdraw it when they feel like, are they even capable of loving at all? Love is by no means unconditional, but there should not be conditions that cause any sort of hurt to the other person.

Along with 'I love you' many women say that their abuser often said 'I'm sorry' when threatened with the idea that the relationship will end. I feel here it is worth reiterating that linguistics have a lot to answer for! What do we as humans understand about the word sorry?

I'm sorry, not sorry

We all may remember a time at school where we were placed in front of someone that had wronged us. An arch nemesis, that we would rather not be friends with, but there we were, standing in front of them, being told to say sorry to each other. But what if we felt we weren't sorry, because it was them that was in the wrong? Why are we told as children to say sorry even if it is not our fault? What meaning does sorry have if we say it even if it was not our fault? We are taught to say sorry, and then we can move on, we can move past the incident and be OK again. Saying sorry just to move forward does not hold the true meaning of what sorry should be. Sorry means, I recognise that I have hurt you and I am remorseful. In an abusive relationship we may have to say sorry to try and move forward or to protect ourselves, but what if we were not the one that needs to be sorry. After an abusive relationship many women overuse the word sorry. I notice that the word sorry is used for very small things that they feel they do wrong. Some have said that they do not know why they say it; others say that they feel deeply remorseful for every small thing they do wrong.

What do we expect from saying sorry? Saying sorry for many is reassurance that it is OK. After an abusive relationship we might be looking for someone just to tell us it is OK. Abusers usually accuse victims of being the ones in the wrong, and the victims tend to believe this. It is rare for an abuser to use the word sorry unless there is a threat that the victim may leave. This may be why we look for acceptance in our actions, we need to be told that it is OK that we do something. I have seen victims use sorry in the following contexts:

- Calling a store: 'sorry, I'm just calling to see if you have something in stock'

- When out with a friend: 'sorry, I need to go to the toilet'

- To let someone, pass: 'sorry, you go first'

- At a restaurant: 'sorry, can I have a glass of water?'

What is the meaning of sorry in each of these contexts? Sorry you're calling a store? But for what for exactly? Are you sorry for them giving you their time? You're sorry you need to visit the loo, but what for though? Are you sorry for your friend having to wait? You're sorry that you are letting someone pass first, but why? Why are you sorry for putting someone before yourself? You're at a restaurant apologising to the waiter because you would like a glass of water. Why are you doing this? If you are in a restaurant, you can ask for a drink and the waiter will bring you one. You are sorry for your existence in most of these examples, but why? Your life matters, you matter, and you are worthy of people's time and effort just as much as anyone else. Keeping track of how often you say sorry can help you to stop saying sorry, you do not need to continuously apologise to others. The word sorry holds a lot of weight for some people, and for others it is just an admittance that you are in the wrong. We look now at how others may view the word sorry.

What does sorry mean to others?

What about if some people view sorry as a word that means I am wrong, and you are right? I share an example below:

A woman opens the door of a shop to walk in, at the same time another woman is walking relatively fast to walk out of the shop. The woman walking in holds the door, but the woman walking out stops quickly glance at something. The woman holding the door then attempts to walk through the door, but they end up crashing in to each other as they both decide to walk through the door at the same time. The woman walking in apologises profusely and the woman walking out says, 'yes, well, I should think so.'

This example can happen in many different situations where you apologise because you want to resolve the issue, even though it is not your fault. This may sometimes be to avoid any sort of conflict as saying sorry to your abuser may have quickly resolved an argument or stopped it from escalating. At times you will be met by someone that will accept the apology and then proceed to make you feel more at fault. Sorry does not really mean I am sorry for my mistake to some people. Sorry is a strong word and evokes different feelings for each of us, and these feelings can even change day to day. The woman who was walking out of the shop could have been looking for medicine for her sick farther that is dying in the most unfair way. You could have been the first person to say sorry to her for many years. Hearing sorry could have shook all things in her that she feels are unfair in her life at this time. This does not excuse people for snapping in this way, especially if it is not your fault. However, this also shows that we should not throw the word sorry around to people who could make us feel worse, especially if we have nothing to be sorry for. If you are a person who says sorry more than a few times a day, look at what sorry means to you. Do not put yourself out there to say sorry if it is not your fault. It is not your fault.

Fairness and Justice in Sorry

What happened to you during your abuse is not fair; it should not have happened to you, and it was wrong. No abuse that happens is fair, but it continues to happen. This is because life is unfair; things happen to people that just do not deserve it. Some people are born in to countries that are unsafe and count days of survival as their wealth. Others are born in to countries that hold unnecessary materials as their wealth. This is how it has been for many years before and this is how it will be for many years to come. Life is not fair. The teacher that asked the two children to say sorry without even knowing who was in the wrong, did this with the idea it was fair. It would have been unfair to punish one in case she chose the wrong one to believe. This is how we as humans see fairness.

In the court system, justice is expected for victims that have been wronged, but evidence is needed to punish someone for their actions.

This sometimes cannot work out as just; sometimes there is just no way that justice can be done. And we as humans are the ones to work out what would be fair justice, but this is subjective to the individual so how can it ever be fair? I might think that a person should be in prison for five years for stealing, but you may think he deserves two. Which one is right? How can we measure fairness and justice if we all have different ideas about what they are?

Justice for being abused does not always happen, up until recent years domestic abuse was extremely hard to prove and convict. With little understanding of it there was less chance that an abuser would be found guilty for what they had done, and coercive control was not a recognised abuse. Many recent victims have been successful in court cases and have received results where their abuser has been sent to prison for a few years. These victims have said that still their abuser did not ever say sorry for what they had done. The word sorry may never have left your abusers mouth, and maybe you feel like that's all you ever needed. Most victims will never get the word sorry from their abusers because they are not sorry. For others that have told me that they got the sorry that they longed for, and do you know what happened? At first some felt angry and others felt safer, but after a while they felt no different; the sorry changed nothing. They had hoped that the words sorry would give closure for their experience and the acknowledgment that their abuse was wrong. But in fact, sorry did not change one thing; they still experienced the symptoms of abuse due to what they had been through. Although being abused was not your fault, sometimes saying sorry to yourself can help to rid guilt that some may carry for their abuse. This guilt is not yours to bear.

So many women, including myself have walked in to a string of abusive relationships when they have been abused once. This can sometimes make it difficult for others to understand, I have heard things from others such as 'well she must be a nightmare to live with if everyone keeps hitting her'. This is extremely unfair considering that perpetrators look for vulnerable women and following an abusive relationship you are exactly that! So far we have looked at what it is to be abused, the ways we can be abused, and it impacts, we take a moment here to look at what a loving relationship looks like.

What is love if it isn't words?

Love is, in simple understanding, a chemical reaction; it's a feeling that happens when these chemicals are released. This understanding of love means that we absolutely can not feel in love with someone 24 hours a day. So, what is love if we don't feel in love all the time? I would like to think that love is:

- Understanding that a person does not have to meet your expectations

- Not placing demands on a person to do as you want them to do

- Accepting the person for who they are, with no intention of changing them for your own benefit

- Being empathic towards a person when they are sharing their feelings with you

- Not controlling the person and accepting that they are free, and that you do not own them

- Not being envious of a person and instead celebrating their successes

- Not self-seeking

- Not throwing mistakes in the person's face; being willing to move forward

- Trusting the person with your feelings

- Being faithful

- Being a team

- Being respectful of each other

- Not using hard words to pull each other down

- Being able to be honest

- Being patient and accepting of faults

- Listening and understanding

- Commitment

- Compromise

- Balance

So, if none of these are present in an abusive relationship, why is it that we stay?

The question of why

Statistics suggest that on average women will experience a dramatic incident up to 35 times before they decide to leave an abusive relationship. (Jaffe, 1982) This statistic gives insight into why some may grow frustrated with the amount of times women return to abusive relationships. This statistic may also explain the reasons why professionals and family members become discouraged when supporting victims. In fact, women often say that on leaving their abuser they find that others are judgmental of the amount of abuse they stood for. Victims have shared that their previous life choices are rarely understood by their family and friends. In most instances this launches the victim into feeling that it is necessary to explain the choices they have made. This can bring a defensive attitude; the victim may feel as though they need to defend their relationship due to the judgments that they face. Why do we expect victims to explain their situations? Why do we judge when we do not know their experience? I answer this with the fact that people judge because they do not understand. Why do we not recognise the life-changing impacts of abuse? I feel we owe it to victims to understand these impacts!

This brings me to a question that is the most frequently asked by others – a question which conjures sickness in the pit of my stomach: 'why didn't you just leave?' If they could have just left as easy as the question rolls off the tongue, don't you think they would have? It is just as small-minded to ask someone who suffers with depression: 'why don't you just be happy?' The explanation to 'why didn't you just leave' is far too complex for victims to be able to give. Most women do not even know themselves why they stayed, because the truth is that they were not able to make their own choices. Instead the answer that is usually given by women is granted the same simplicity as the question, this answer is: 'I love him'.

Domestic abuse does not exclude any type of person from its grasp; no one is exempt from the possibility that they might enter in to an abusive relationship. Why does domestic abuse take hold of so many lives? Maybe the question 'why didn't you just leave?' is asked from a genuine curiosity, for the unknown that we seek to desperately understand. But when victims are asked this question, I have witnessed their eyes glaze over as if they are searching their soul for the real answers. This question seems to exacerbate all negative feelings that an abused person holds about their experiences. They feel judged in their choices to stay, which makes them question themselves as a person.

There are some set answers that apply to this question, the abuse may have been specific to the individual, but some answers will be similar. These answers should be common knowledge to anyone supporting a victim, there is no doubt that domestic abuse needs to be better understood. The journey through this book answers the question of 'why' repeatedly to show how many influences there are as to why someone stays. Maybe you will find the answers as to why you yourself stayed.

An image of a relationship with physical abuse gives most people cause to question why someone would ever return to a violent other. It is simplistic to say that if you were in this relationship you would just leave. No victims return with the idea that they will be hurt again, many believe that their partner has changed. They believe that the human element in their partner will feel remorseful about their actions, that they will return to a person who is sorry. This is usually the case but for some victims the perpetrator has used threats that have been scary enough to make them go back. If it was only physical abuse it would be so much easier to leave. But as previously noted physical abuse is never the only form of abuse that a person will experience. In all aspects of domestic abuse there are levels of control that exist in the relationship. We return to the idea of being brainwashed and controlled in chapter 3. But first we explore what I feel is, the most studied ideas in social developmental Psychology. This idea suggests that we are mainly a product of our environment and that our childhood is the causal factor in how we develop relationships in our future. I explore this area with caution as I myself, believe that you do not have to have had a bad childhood to become the victim of abuse. However, I do acknowledge that there is a higher chance that you may enter in to a bad relationship if your experiences in life have been negative. I ended an extremely violent relationship and entered in to one that was more psychologically abusive. I thought that in comparison to violence, the next relationship was good.

The general knowledge regarding domestic abuse is that there is a cycle of abuse through childhood to adult hood, but this should not be considered the norm. I know many women that have had an extremely good upbringing and they have still become the victims of domestic abuse. Victims of abuse have explained that they felt judged by their background when they have disclosed their abuse to professionals. Subjective writing from a victim explains that rather than looking to understand how she felt about her abuse professionals looked at her background as an inevitable factor of her abuse. (Sweetnam, 2013) I feel that it is clear now that I do not support that a negative upbringing is the only reason why women get in to an abusive relationship. However, we acknowledge it here because for some women this will be relevant. If you feel that your upbringing was good, and your family influences will not have shaped any vulnerabilities then you are invited to skip this chapter. Chapter 3 may bring more insight to the reasons why you became abused and why you chose to stay.

What do some psychologists say about upbringing?

Whether you are a parent or not you can you use this idea to ask questions about your own parents' styles of interactions with you. Can you think of anything that your parents continuously did or said that may have shaped the way you are today? Unfortunately, we all have human error, so I imagine there will be a time you can relay where your parents may have not reacted in a way that was helpful. I myself am a parent and I can say as a parent we make choices and sometimes these may not be the best ones. No parent or care giver can get it right 100% of the time.

When I was pregnant my midwife told me not to be anxious. I questioned her on why I should try to be less anxious. Her answer was: 'because your mood effects the baby, if you're anxious then so are they.' Imagine for a minute the level of anxiety, depression and worries a soon to be mother may feel in an abusive relationship. What would the baby be feeling? Was this you as a baby? The midwife made me realise that the baby lives in you and it is therefore obvious that they will be affected by what you feel. My midwife also explained that babies in the womb become aware of familiar voices and what tones these voices have. In domestically abusive relationships these familiar voices and tones may be negative, loud and abrupt. If this is the normal style of tones that we hear it is obvious that we will be affected by this style of interaction. The potential influence of this could be that in the womb we are becoming a person who is more anxious, or we are becoming someone who believes that negative interactions are normal.

So, what happens when you are born in to an abusive home? Maybe your mother is preoccupied with arguing with your father and you are not involved in it but are witnessing it. As we grow, we need back and forth communication to show we are acknowledged. We can't yet talk, we rely on face-to-face contact, so we can take in facial expressions and lip movements. This interaction not only teaches us how to shape words but obviously shows us how to engage in a conversation. The 'you go, now I go' dynamics of any type of conversation. A study that highlights this was carried out by Provenzi et al, (2018) Provenzi researched the effects of mother and infant interactions. It was found that Infants who experienced more attuned mothering had a higher IQ, better behaviour, and greater ability to develop good relationships with others. This study shows that infants who do not have much acknowledgment from their parent are likely to have less social and cognitive skills than a child who does.

Provenzi et al, (2018) also founded that children who were not shown any remorse from their mother should she have upset them were more likely to have higher cortisol reactivity. Cortisol is the chemical that is released when we are in a state of anxiety, years ago it would be cortisol that would have given us enough energy to run from a tiger. But for a child sitting in a classroom or a victim of abuse sitting in a chair, this energy can be unmanageable. Many of the children and victims of abuse that I work with seem to be in a high state of anxiety, they find it difficult to concentrate and they say that school work can become impossible to understand.

Growing up we take all our visual surroundings in; we examine others and judge if they are safe. I recall that a playgroup I once worked at was full of children that peek at the world from behind their mothers' legs. On their first day most infants seemed more scared and assessed their surroundings before leaving their mothers. So, I imagine that a small baby who is visually taking in the world around them is constantly assessing situations. If you are a baby who is sitting on the sofa caught up in one of your mum and dads' arguments, you are likely to be taking in all the visual things that are happening. Assessing movements and tone of voice may help you to asses if the situation is safe or unsafe. Can you think of a time where you have had to take in all visual surroundings in this way? Maybe you watched a scary film and were then scared of the dark afterwards? You know that being in this mode makes you feel anxious, on high alert, so that if anything bad should happen you can run away. Can you imagine how this might be the same for a baby who is growing up in a house where there is abuse? Do you think they are likely to either become someone who will accept that this is how people communicate? Do you think that they could become more anxious as a person?

I have worked with many children who have grown up in an abusive home that do not know how to start or maintain a conversation with others. They fail to start conversations because they feel they won't be accepted or heard in an interaction. Looking again at the research findings from Provenzi et al, (2018) it was found that forming positive relationships (attachments) with others, was probable to be poorer in infants who had a less consistent style of parenting influences. A person who has grown up in an abusive household may not have been acknowledged as a child as their parents were preoccupied with arguing. Mcadams et al (2017) showed that parent affection and attachment are likely to be linked to adolescent self-worth. Although generally confident people can also become victims of abuse, I have noticed that there are a much higher number of victims that say that they have never been confident. And if this is not the case, they say that they have now become unconfident by their experiences of abuse. Some women are vulnerable because of their upbringing but others that are not vulnerable can still become abused although it is less likely. I feel this may be because abusers like to pray on people that are vulnerable, and a more confident person will be harder to control than one that is already accepting of negative treatment.

Using the findings from the research noted above, we now highlight the type of person that has been negatively affected by experiencing unattuned mothering or witnessing abuse. This person may develop in to Person 1:

Person 1 (victim): *I am not worthy, I won't bother expressing upset because I don't have good communication skills, I won't have my emotional needs met, I want to please others.*

If you have witnessed or experienced abuse in the home, you may be more likely to think this is the norm because this is all you know. Your boundaries on danger are formed and this may mean that you accept low levels of safety as good enough. Although the research mentioned in this chapter does show higher probability of these predictions, this is not to say that every child from an abused home will become an abuser or a victim of abuse. We look now in more at perpetrators.

Some women have reported that their abuser has left them and got with another partner with as little time as one day! We look here at why this might happen and try to make sense of how someone can just choose to move on so easily.

Perpetrators of abuse

If you are viewed as a product that is there to bring happiness, what happens when you don't bring happiness? The same thing that happens to an empty packet of sweets: you are thrown away. And what will this person need to feel happy again? A new bag of sweets.

Some perpetrators can move on quickly, which is difficult to accept if you still believe the words that they wooed you with. How do you feel when you are an empty bag of sweets and someone else is a brand-new full bag? Not great! In fact, maybe you question your worth: an empty bag of sweets is worth nothing. What has happened does not mean that you are worth nothing, the problem is not you, the problem is that the abuser can not place value on people.

When a relationship like this ends abruptly it can be difficult to process that they may not have loved you like you thought they did.

Some perpetrators are unaware of their abusive behaviours; others know that they are abusive. I have met many perpetrators who think that their behaviour is acceptable because this is what they are used to. A study carried out by Sousa et al, (2010) showed that children who are exposed to domestic abuse are more likely to act in antisocial behaviour, risky behaviour or violence. This could support that abusers have themselves been victim to an upbringing of abuse.

From working with victims, I have noted 2 different types of perpetrator that are commonly described. The first type of perpetrator can adapt and change their personalities to suit others. They can be charming, controlling and manipulative. These types of people quickly evaluate what you like so that they can be the person you have always wanted. They are a chameleon and intend on becoming who you desire so that you see them as important, valuable and needed. Their chameleon like ways eventually leave you feeling confused about who they are. When this person is recognised as being adaptive, the front is broken, and they may feel exposed and challenged, the abuse can get worse and less concealed. It is important to note here that questioning someone on how they act is within your right in a relationship. A person who becomes abusive when questioned is a perpetrator and it is not your fault for questioning their actions.

The second type of perpetrator I have noted is the kind that has the background of being fairly spoiled as a child, this is not to say that all spoiled children will be perpetrators. However, I have noted that this type of perpetrator has a background where they have been given more than they need in many ways. This type of person is usually not aware of the abuse they carry out on others, and this puzzled me for a while as to why. A recent study has found that overvaluation from parents can cause someone to become narcissistic. Overvaluation causes the child to view they have more privileges and that they are superior to others. (Brummelman et al, 2015)

Many victims who have had an abuser with this background have said that their abuser was always seen as a 'golden boy' to their family. That their actions were never viewed as wrong but rather his family stood by him and accused the victim of provoking him. A person who would have been cared for in this way may be unable to regulate negative emotions and will always want things their own way. It is obvious that a child that never has been spoiled would not have had chance to feel many negative emotions. Due to not being able to hold negative emotions they may react with anger to anything that makes them feel remotely sad. They may never have been challenged or questioned, which means they won't be receptive to any negativity directed towards them. This kind of perpetrator has been described similarly to a Narcissist, they do not care for others, they are arrogant, jealous, can't be happy for others and deflect any negative accusations. (BBC radio 4, 2019) Victims have said that when questioned their abusers have accused them of being paranoid, mad or psycho for saying anything negative about them.

Some perpetrators have the awareness and empathy to change and are willing to learn how to change. However, some may never truly love someone as they do themselves. A spoiled perpetrator is likely to be impatient, unaware, arrogant and have high expectations for others to meet their needs.

Looking at the idea of perpetrator and victims thus far how can it seem like these two people fall in love? What is it about this type of relationship that may be fuelling the need to stay? We look at one possible causal factor here:

How can this feel like love?

Let's look again at person 1 that was mentioned earlier:

Person 1 (victim): *I am not worthy, I won't bother expressing upset because I don't have good communication skills, I won't have my emotional needs met, I want to please others.*

Now let's remind ourselves about the golden boy type of perpetrator:

Person 2 (perpetrator): *I am the only one of importance, people need to please me, I won't accept any type of compromise, I need others to work around my needs.*

When we compare what each of these people need from others, we see that both are getting what they are used to. Person 1 feels unworthy and that they need to please others, and person 2 feels important and thinks others are there to please them. Person 1 thinks this is what they are worth and does not see that person 2 is unreasonable because this treatment is normal to them. So, these two types of people could come together and meet each other's needs, despite it being a negative relationship. When we look at the victim and perpetrator type of relationship in this way, it is easier to see how perpetrators may prefer vulnerable women. This would support how so many vulnerable women continue to enter in to an abusive relationships. The research presented in this chapter suggests that unattuned mothering can cause cognitive and social delays, then these delays lead to a higher chance of risky behaviours and violence. This could be a high predictor that a child may become a perpetrator of abuse. Non attuned mothering is also suggested to cause low-self-worth which is present in victims that are abused. To highlight the cycle that has been show by the research explained in this chapter see this diagram:

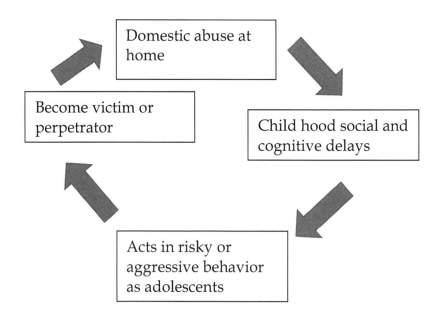

Knowing how the past can influence the now can partly answer the question of 'why didn't you just leave?'. Many psychologists suggest that our past experiences have a lot to do with the way in which we develop. If you have never trusted any one with your safety then you may not have ever known how to trust, your first step to trusting others is to first trust yourself. Weather the cycle above is relevant to you or not, trust is still an issue following an abusive relationship. Trusting yourself is not an easy task after an abusive relationship. Many people may question your choices so it may become difficult to not question them yourself.

Acknowledging how victims may accept abuse as the norm is important but this does not mean that confident happy people will not be abused, nor does it mean that every person with low self-worth will be abused. I do not like to attribute past relationships as a predictor of future relationships, but they at least must be acknowledged as one possible factor of why we may accept abuse. The next chapter looks at a different approach on abuse, this is underpinned by the idea that anyone can be brain washed regardless of their upbringing. I propose that our attachment to people can be made from fear and the need for survival, despite what your past relations have been.

Chapter 3

Attachment Capture Syndrome ... can I be free?

I guess he wants me to stay here forever

We need people to realise this stuff!

There is no known mental health issue that looks at the impacts of abuse as one collective. However, I have worked with hundreds of victims who experience the same set of issues or have exacerbated issues by experiencing abuse. Victims often receive more than one diagnosis to label the impacts of their abuse. Not only do victims receive multiple diagnoses, but in some instances the impacts of abuse are not even considered at all. A high number of midwifery students suggested that they have never seen anyone in their practice that displayed issues connected with domestic abuse. More senior midwifes say that they have seen many women who have displayed issues connected with domestic abuse. (Bradbury-Jones & Broadhurst, 2015) This is quite worrying considering the number of women who must attend hospital due to domestic abuse injuries. I feel that this highlights that newer health professionals without experience do not have guidelines of what to look out for in abuse victims. This suggests that we need to have a recognised set of symptoms that are clearly linked to experiences of abuse.

Other health care providers have treated psychological and physical symptoms of domestic abuse as symptoms of stress. Although women attribute their psychological and physical symptoms to their experiences of domestic abuse. (Abbot et al, 1995) Many victims have been diagnosed with complex trauma, which is a specific type of post-traumatic stress. The symptoms for this include:

- Shame

- Guilt

- Emotional difficulties

- Low concentration

- Cutting family and friends off

- Acting in risky behaviours

- Suicidal thoughts

Many victims I have worked with have been diagnosed with borderline personality disorder (BPD) due to their dependent relationship with their idealised partner in which boundaries are not recognised. (Zanarini et al, 1990). People with this disorder can display the following symptoms:

- Little ability to tolerate frustration

- Not learn from mistakes

- Unstable relationships

- Unstable self-image

- Emotional swings

- Feeling of emptiness

- Reckless behaviour

- Dependency issues

The issues above could be seen in many victims that have experienced domestic abuse. Most victims I have worked with that have BPD have said that their issues only surfaced following their abusive relationship; this to me suggested that something else might be happening here. Mary Zanarini (1990) studied BPD and the presence of certain issues that come with it. This study showed that 80% of borderline patients had trouble tolerating aloneness, suffered from abandonment and annihilation concerns. I would say it is normal to feel like you can not be alone after domestic abuse. Many women say that they do not like to be alone as this allows them to be in their thoughts about the past, or that they fear protecting themselves when they are alone. The sense of abandonment is likely to be present in victims of abuse as they may have been isolated from their family and friends or felt more withdrawn. Annihilation concerns may be present in so many victims as they fear that their abuser will destroy them. Some start to worry about their ex-partner finding ways to destroy them, and some of these ideas are not always logical. This suggests to me that following an abusive relationship the feeling of being unsafe is severe. If so, many mental health symptoms are present after experiencing abuse it is no wonder why victims are being diagnosed with many different diagnoses.

So, does this mean that most victims also have BPD? or does this mean that many victims have not got BPD but are being diagnosed with it because the symptoms are the same. This could suggest fault with the way in which abuse victims are labelled following an abusive relationship. I feel that victims are categorised with different types of mental health issues because there is not one label that recognises all the symptoms that occur following abuse. Because of this, many victims are diagnosed with all the mental health issues mentioned above. With so many different diagnoses, victims can feel that they are broken, too broken to be fixed. For some the diagnosis of their many mental health labels is too much for them to overcome and they have resided in the fact that this is now them. They feel that they 'are' their diagnosis that they have been labelled, and this is now their identity. If the impacts of domestic abuse were looked at as a collective, the diagnosis of some of these issues could be rolled into one. This would at least give victims the knowledge that this is a reaction to their abuse and is not their own self.

One of the most interesting symptoms that is both present in BPD and following abuse is the dependency issue. I have worked with so many victims that have shown a dependency and idealisation towards their abuser. It's almost as if you become half a person because you take on your abusers' thoughts and react and act how they want you to. You are a puppet, and without your puppeteer you don't really know what to do or how to live.

On finding the similarities with the impacts of abuse and BPD I reviewed many research papers that evaluated these symptoms. I was Specifically interested in the bond and attachment that a victim still has to their abuser. One research paper written by Biederman (Biderman, 1957; Farber et al, 1957) investigated American prisoners of war that were brainwashed by their captors. This paper gave me the most clear-cut findings that mimic the tactics of an abuser and the impacts of these tactics on their victim. This research shows that there are set tactics that are used to have certain impacts on others! This to me shows that no one person is exempt from being of sound mind following this style of treatment. This to me answers in black and white the question, 'why does she stay!'

TACTIC	IMPACT
Isolation	Makes victim dependant on interrogator
Monopolises perception (controls thoughts and opinions)	Makes victims focus only on what the interrogator thinks. Changes their own views to the same views as interrogator
Prolonged interrogation	Weakens victim's mental ability to resist. (They give in to what interrogator wants)

or questioning	
Threats	Creates anxiety in the victim, which makes them conform
Occasional indulgence (occasional niceness)	Gives positive motivation to comply with what the interrogator wants with the hopes of receiving good treatment
Omnipotence (makes themselves seem inferior)	Makes victim feel inferior so that it seems more pointless to resist
Degradation	Reduces person to feeling less valued. This also makes the idea of resistance feel more damaging than worth it
Enforcing trivial demands	Develops routine of compliance to enforced rules

These findings show that these specific types of abuse over a lengthy period can change people's mindset. All the above tactics can be likened to what perpetrators do to their victims. And as the table shows, the symptoms of abuse are the same in how victims feel during and after the abuse. This is a scary finding considering that war tactics are used specifically to enforce control and pain on others. The prisoners feel completely dependent and controlled by their captors which suggests that they do not have free will to think for themselves anymore even if they were free to do so. While victims are often told they are depressed or anxious it must be considered that tactics such as this are likely to cause unstable mental wellbeing. It is as if the abuser has temporarily captured the victims being and the victim no longer operates as an independent person with free will to think.

I carried out a study with 100 women who have experienced abuse, I gained access to these women through a domestic abuse Charity called Calan DVS. All women were abuse free for a minimum of 6 months and had experienced abuse with in the last 5 years. The women completed a questionnaire of what symptoms they have experienced following their abuse. From the symptoms women reported I created a list of symptoms that over 85% of women experienced.

The symptoms that effected 85% or over are as follows:

- Low concentration 86%

- Emotional swings 87%

- Dependency issues 85%

- Loss of ability to express emotions 89%

- Feelings of guilt 85%

- Low mood 89%

- Nervous/anxious/heightened stress 93%

- Loss of identity 92%

- Loss of confidence 96%

- Feeling alone 92%

- Hold negative views about yourself 91%

- Still feel attached to ex-partner 85%

- Difficulty making decisions 89%

This is a big list of issues that could be used to suggest that this is someone with depression, anxiety, PTSD, or BPD. I feel that it would benefit victims to be able to recognise that these symptoms are all issues that are likelier to be caused by one factor. I have termed these collective issues as 'Attachment capture syndrome'.

We look here at the importance of this syndrome being commonly recognised.

Attachment Capture Syndrome

The moment that I knew I had to try and change things for victims was while I was supporting a woman who had been violently attacked by the father of her child. I attended a review of this victims' case with many professionals and the presence of the victim. One professional turned to the victim and said with haste: 'You failed to keep yourself safe the night of the attack.' I felt compelled to scream at everyone in the room: 'Don't you know how abuse works? Don't you know what has happened in the wiring of her brain?'. But I did not shout either question; instead I interjected with the impacts of domestic abuse and did not stop explaining until everyone got it. I started to wonder how many other victims have been blamed or judged in these situations. How many other women have had their personality captured by a man, to the point where they do not recognise themselves as independent anymore. I feel that it is necessary for not just professionals but for everyone to understand that when you leave an abusive relationship, you do not become a competent independent thinker straight away. You need time to start to think on your own again, time to know what is safe and unsafe and time to think about what is wrong and right. All these views have been slowly changed by your abuser, and it will take time for you to put everything back in to perspective. We need to fully understand the tactics that are imposed on victims so that we understand why they return to their abuser. In doing this we can begin to look at how to unpick the control and dominance that the perpetrator has had and empower the victims to move forward.

Many victims of abuse feel alone in their experiences. And, putting it bluntly, they are! This is because no one truly understands! This feeling of aloneness often bonds them with their abuser even more, as they can sometimes feel that this is the only other person that understands their experiences. It is detrimental to victims of abuse that symptoms are better understood by others. This will help their family and supporting professionals to acknowledge the changes that they have experienced. From my experience the most common symptom that is misunderstood by others is the bond that victims have with their abuser. It was highlighted above that certain abusive tactics will influence this bond. This bond in my opinion is also present because the victim and perpetrator are the only two people that experience the abuse.

Victims are often told things like: 'it's OK, now you're safe'; 'he's gone now so you can move on, your free'. Moving on may feel impossible when your ability to make decisions has been captured by your ex-partner. Explaining your abuse to others can usually be met with the conclusion that your abuser is a terrible person. This judgment can make it ever so difficult if you still feel loss for this person. I promise that it is normal after an abusive relationship to ask yourself, 'why am I still dependant?, why am I still scared?' Many victims try and hide the fact that they are still dependant on their partner, and why wouldn't they when they are judged on their previous choices to stay. Why wouldn't they if others conclude that he was terrible, and they are free now he has gone. Even if this attachment is not a loving attachment, victims usually still have a dependency on their abuser because they controlled how they lived.

This again is even more reason to acknowledge that Attachment Capture Syndrome is the result of domestic abuse.

Some of the most common symptoms I have recognised in victims of abuse are explored in more depth here:

Loss of identity

Loss of identity can make it hard to do anything at all; this is because you may not know what you want. The tactics of war explored above show that victims take on their captors' views. This inevitably causes victims to be less able to think for themselves. If you have been unable to express yourself, you will be less able to make your own choices on who you are and what you think. The social aspect of who we are helps to shape our identity because we confirm this by giving our opinions and thoughts to others. Who we are socially can only be developed with socialising with others. In this interaction we gain other perspectives and tend to interrogate these with our own views. Being isolated from others you are unable to speak as you want and are unable to continue activities that define you. Loss of identity can leave you feeling hopeless and unaware of where you are going in life. After domestic abuse many women say that the things, they used to do, do not bring them pleasure anymore, and it is therefore even harder to be who they once were. You may never feel like you did before, you may never want to do the things you did that defined you. Knowing who you are may seem like an unachievable task after abuse, but rest assured this is common.

Heightened stress

When you are in a state of heightened stress you might experience the following:

- Sweating
- Alertness
- Overthinking
- Headaches
- Shaking
- Loss of sleep
- Fatigue

- Tiredness

- Loss of appetite

- Feeling worried

- Unable to cope

- Poor memory or unable to concentrate

These symptoms could make it difficult for you to feel any energy at all. (If you are worried that these symptoms are not due to your abuse you should visit your doctor.)

Loss of confidence

Loss of confidence can affect everything about you and the way you interact with others. Loss of confidence can make you feel judged, even to the point where you may worry about being in a big shopping queue with other people. Confidence is knowing that you are worthy, able and valued as a person. Maybe you are someone that has always lacked in confidence. If so, then I ask why? Why is it that you are unconfident? Is there anything you can do that would make you feel more achieved or confident in yourself? Confidence can take a while to develop, and some people will always fear what others think. Loss of confidence is a problem if it prevents you from doing the things you want or need to do.

Confidence is not something that you can gain overnight but it can be gained by making mini achievements. This could be by acknowledging the things that you feel unconfident in. In your notebook plan out the small goal that you would like to achieve. Use the questions below to plan the situation:

Task

1. Plan a day and time where you can realistically do this task
2. Write down all your potential worries about doing this task
3. Write down all logical explanations that go against your perceived worries
4. Has there been a time where you have been able to do this task?

> 5. Make a safety plan around your worries; for example, this may be to tell someone where you are/have someone's number on speed dial if you get worried/work out how you can get of the situation of you need to.

The idea that you can't do things like socialise because you worry what others will think of you is crippling. When I myself experienced social anxiety, I was once told by my counsellor: 'What makes you think you're so important that other people will care what you are doing?' This sentence angered me, and I was insulted at the time, but if we really think about this advice, it's true. Everyone has busy lives and to think that people will be that interested in what you say or what you do is almost egotistical. You may want to put this book down at this point or throw it at the wall; I know I would have if I had a book when I was told this by the counsellor!

Lack of confidence is not only when we feel judged by others, because from being abused it seems that we can become our biggest critic. We become so judgmental of ourselves, just like our abuser was, this could highlight how much we took on his views as our own, much like the prisoners of war we looked at previously. It is OK to fail at things, it is OK to have made mistakes, it is OK to accept that we are not always right, because none of us are!

It is likely that if someone is in a shopping queue, mocking you, they themselves feel useless. Next time you feel judged by someone, imagine how they might feel? Is this something that is their own issue?

Feeling alone

Feeling alone after abuse is normal; despite being in an unhealthy relationship you have still lost a spouse. The person that you shared your life with has gone. Even if they weren't a nice person, they were still there, and now they are not. Domestic abuse is confusing because on one hand you are safe and are free to heal, but at the same time you may still experience grief for the loss of your relationship. It might be helpful to acknowledge both feelings; you may still need time to grieve for the person that is no longer in your life. Just know that this person is no longer in your life because they were unhealthy for you.

From working with clients, I see that the feelings of being alone are real! You are alone in your experiences because maybe everyone close to you does not understand what you have been through. This can make you feel disconnected to the world or stop you from wanting to connect to others. Others may not understand what you have been through and say things that make you feel worse. The thing is, not many people know how to interact with someone who has experienced abuse, not only because they don't understand it but because they don't know how to offer comfort. Knowing that people do not understand might make it easier to not be affected by what they say.

I conclude this chapter with the need for Attachment Capture Syndrome to be more recognised. If this was the case then we would not be in a position where others would judge us from a place of non-understanding.

Chapter 4

Rewire your brain

Like mamma said, follow your heart but take your brain with you

Control of the youthful brain is easier to capture

Many women begin to get into a relationship before they are 20 years of age. This is not an issue if the person you are with is not an abuser. I remember developing between 16-19 years of age and like most other teens I knew, I was unsure of who I was and more easily influenced by the opinions of others. I have noticed that a lot of the adolescents that I work with, find it extremely important to be liked and to fit in to their social group. At this age I have noted that their views seem to easily be shaped into what fits with others; some seem to be less confident to think opposing views. In these cases, I have found that their identity is shaped by other people, which has led to many young victims of abuse struggling to find who they really are. I feel that it is so much more difficult to know yourself when your views have never been your own.

Many women feel completely lost without their abuser, and this could be partly due to the example above which shows that they have not really made their own opinions. We could also say that if your views have never been your own then they could be more easily changed by an abuser.

<u>Our brains kind of tick us!</u>

The above notion can be used to suggest that this may be another example of how people can become dependent on their abuser. I feel that if we know the reasons why we are dependant we can then start to become independent. Looking at the bond between victim and perpetrator it can be viewed as something strong … too strong to break without help. Domestic abuse does not only happen to people that have had bad childhoods. There is something else that happens that bonds people together despite their past. In an abusive relationship you have seen parts of each other's behaviours that you wouldn't want anyone else to see. You have been through something so horrific together that in a strange way it bonds you in ways that you couldn't ever begin to explain to someone. This is because, tactics have been used to make you feel this way, you become dependent.

<u>We are just science</u>

We are science – we are made of just a pile of scientific chemical stuff – so it's kind of good to know what is happening inside of us when we feel connection and love. When you fall in love you experience feelings due to the chemicals, dopamine, oxytocin and adrenaline. Dopamine and oxytocin are the feel-good chemicals which make you feel fuzzy and in love, and adrenaline gives you that flustered flutter that you feel. (BBC Science, 2014) So, here's the ridiculous part: when you are arguing stressed or in a conflicting position you also produce adrenaline. (BBC Science, 2013) Here we see that love and conflict both release adrenaline which could support the reasons why we get confused.

So …from what this tells me is that your brain is basically unaware of what the appropriate reaction is all it knows is that it wants more adrenaline! Going from a relationship that was fuelled with stress to not having this must deplete the amount of adrenaline that you have. Some victims say that they experience withdrawal symptoms such as needing an argument to happen, which I really feel could be due to the need for adrenaline. If this is the case it is no wonder, why some women feel that they need to be back with their abuser. Basically, you need to teach your body not to love drama. We look now at the infinite circles of abuse which is a pattern I have recognised in so many patterns of abusive relationships. If you imagine the need for adrenaline, this is yet another factor why women choose to stay with an abuser. As we have explored this book so far, we begin to see that there are many factors at play in an abusive relationship. It is not as simple as people may presume. The circles below show how we can come to accept being in this pattern of adrenaline and apologies, repeatedly.

The infinite circles of abuse

We are all individual but on some scientific levels we are the same. Let's look at the infinite circles of abuse to see why we accept abuse as OK even though we know deep down it is not. Going back to the question: why doesn't she just leave? I know even victims have asked themselves this at times. But the truth is, the relationship may not have been bad all the time; in fact, at times it may even be the best relationship you have ever had. See the next page for the infinite circles:

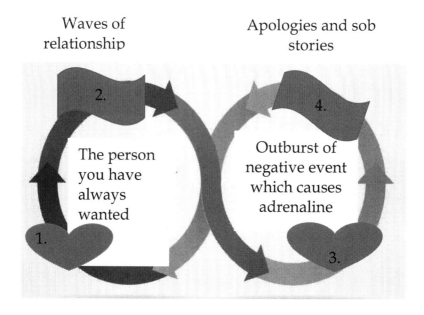

Waves of relationship

Apologies and sob stories

2.

4.

The person you have always wanted

Outburst of negative event which causes adrenaline

1.

3.

While you are in stage 1, the abuser is the perfect person, everything you want, the best person you have ever met. When you are in stage 2 everything will be calm for a while, days, weeks or maybe months. Stage 3 will follow where there will be an outburst, a negative event. At this point you may think: why don't I just leave? This is the beginning of stage 4 where the re-building of the relationship starts, and your partner is apologetic; maybe they go back and forth between 'it's your fault/my fault'. It doesn't take long before they are back in stage 1 and they are again the perfect person and you remember all the good in that person. At this point it seems less attractive to leave because you believe that they are everything you want.

I question whether the perfect person truly exists or is this a persona that abusers can use when they want to manipulate their partners. Is it more conscious than unconscious? A person that displays abusive behaviours is usually very self-centred and cannot see other's points of view. They do not care about other's feelings or experiences. The infinity circles suggest that an abusive relationship can be relatively good; the victim will therefore always hold on to a time where they had the perfect partner.

As humans some of us have the need to help others. In stage 4 perpetrators may tell us how bad their lives are and how their past was terrible. Some victims have said they knew somewhere in them that the way their partner treated them was wrong, but their empathy for their partners experience encouraged them to help. This can be explained easily with how we sometimes want to sponsor a good cause, even though you don't really have that much money to spare. Your gut instinct tells you not to sponsor them, but your feelings override that, and you end up with a monthly direct debit. These overwhelming feelings are often found in people that have a need to help others, so how does this work out in relationships? We look at this in the next section.

Use your brain not your feelings

Most abusers don't come in to victims' lives shouting and screaming, they often come in on a white horse with no alarm bells ringing. They seem to test the water before they become abusive and at first, they need to be, as noted above, 'the person you have always wanted'. They may start to look for sympathy from their victim, to work out how much they can take advantage of this person. People who are natural caregivers or rescuers, in my opinion, seem to be more likely to look at broken people as a project of potentials. The need to help is innate in some people and this can lead to wanting to support some one that is abusive. The problem with this is that broken people usually can not be saved by someone else; this must come from themselves.

If you are a person that can relate to the cycle of abuse, then you yourself may be broken. You can not expect that someone will be good for you, if you are not good for you. For all women in general, I ask you, how do we choose partners? If there are men in shining armour and white horses that seem to be what we want, how can we decipher between perpetrators and genuinely nice men? As crazy as it sounds, we kind of need to know them inside out before getting in to a relationship with them. I have a confession to make which may make me sound crazy myself! Following 2 abusive relationships, I was determined that I would never get in to one again. I promised myself that I would not become serious with anyone unless I felt that I knew them well enough to judge if they were an abuser. I wrote down questions in my diary when I started dating again. Both previous relationships had happened fast with out me really asking my self the right questions about these people. Ill share these with you later but first we explore 'tick lists.'

A relationship that is always good is a big ask as relationships that are healthy are also filled with negative experiences. I have heard many women's dating tick lists: they search for a tall, handsome and rich man. This is what they search for because this is what they feel will make them happy. You may need a tall man because you would like to feel small, so is this an insecurity that could be excluding you from the short love of your life! If someone handsome is just that, what will happen when beauty fades and you are left with someone who you dislike as a person. Money may bring you happiness and a stress-free life for a while, but will this help you to feel connected to someone? What will this eventually do for your self-worth? Can you achieve happiness with another person if your tick list is nothing to do with who they are? What are you searching for?

<u>What are we searching for?</u>
<u>The bad boy</u>

I have heard the age-old story of 'I love a bad boy'. I too was disillusioned into thinking I wanted this. Having a bad boy is almost like being with someone famous; no one will stand up to him. Everyone knows him and fears him and there is a certain amount of respect from others when they see him. Being with a man like this eventually encourages others to view you like this by association. People start asking 'are you (name of abuser)'s misses?' And there it is: you have a level of importance from people and this makes you feel safe. But how contradictory that you are in the most dangerous position you could be. People do not respect this person. They fear him; this is not respect. Being with this person brings feelings of safety but you only need to have heard the story to know: bad boys are going to be bad to you too.

Why is it that we love a bad boy? I have searched long and hard for this answer and the closest thing I can fathom is again by taking it back to basics. Years ago, we would have wanted to be with the most savage man, the biggest man, and why? Well, because they would hunt the most food, they can protect us from danger, and they look healthy enough to give strong healthy children. The perfect genes, right? I ask what if we have evolved to some extent, but still our brains are stuck in this simplistic type of selection. Whether he is strong should not matter; whether he is a savage bad boy should not matter.

I suggest that kindness is what we must search for. How does he treat other women? What does he think of his mother? Does he speak with kindness? Does he hold good morals? Or has he begged, cheated and stole in his savage unevolved ways. You can change the cycle; we hold the power to choose savages or New Age men. For the sake of your own safety and the future of humanity, leave the bad boys alone.

Humour

Some of us search for humour as a trait we want in others. I feel that humour is often a trait that is associated with intellect, but what we find humorous is different for many of us. School children bully each other to make their friends laugh; they will think nothing of embarrassing someone in order to gain popularity. Ridicule is not humour, yet I have heard so many women say that they found the abuser's jokes funny when he ridiculed others. How is this any different to bullying at school? Shouldn't we be a bit more developed than this as adults? Making fun of people is not only a low form of wit, it is also a telling sign of a person's internal monologue. We have already explored that people who ridicule others are holding deep-seated negative views about themselves. I have spent many years listening to people ridicule others, and it was always apparent that the things they ridicule were also present in themselves. Using ridicule is a way of hiding how you feel about negative views on yourself. (S., Freud, 1905) The person that feels stupid will mock people who are clever as well as mock people who they consider to be less intelligent than them. They feel that this deflects away from the fact they have insecurities about their intellect. This style of deflection is just not funny so why do some people think ridicule is humorous. This is bullying not humour; let's leave this at the playground.

I am whoever I tell you I am, right?

I know that we tend to search for kindness in others and some people like to tell us that they are kind. 'I am kind … I am kind … I am kind … did I mention I am kind; do you think I'm kind yet? If someone protests that they are a certain kind of person, this can usually mean that they are not. 'The lady doth protest too much' was a line written in a William Shakespeare play to insinuate that an actress was being insincere. (W., Shakespeare, 1914) I feel this line speaks truth: if someone tells you repeatedly with conviction that they are kind, it isn't necessarily true. We can recognise kindness with the gestures people make, with the acknowledgment of your feelings, with the way that they act. Words mean nothing if the actions are not there to back it up. You should not need to protest that you are kind, if you *are* kind.

We also have expectancies of how others should treat us. Some one maybe funny and kind, but their traits are sometimes not enough. We have seen how some perpetrators view victims as products, but this idea is also present with the way we expect others to meet our needs. While we should have a level of respect and attention from our loved ones, we also should realise that we can not make people live up to our high expectations.

What do you Expect?

Many of us have different values, which mean we have different ideas about how we treat others and how we should be treated. When entering a relationship, it is important to look at the other person's values as well as your own. There must be an understanding of what each other's expectancies are and how these expectancies fit with your comfort zone. If you are in a relationship where the other person has high expectancies that you find difficult to meet, this can turn in to an unhealthy relationship. People show love in different ways, and sometimes because of this, we fail to recognise what the other person does for us. If you speak a different kind of love to your partner, it is necessary to know how you appreciate, understand and value each other. We may be creating our own heartache with the expectancy that others speak the same language of love as we do. So what language of love do you speak and what kind of love do you value most?

Time

Time is something that is usually a valued entity in a relationship, this is because without quality time, the relationship may not progress. Some people hold time in more demand than others, so here the balance in time is necessary. It is important to recognise what is healthy quality time, and what is demanding too much time. If someone is demanding of your time then you can start to feel stifled, this quickly becomes overwhelming. I have worked with some victims who were made to face time their partners while they were out shopping as their partner wanted to know where they were all the time. This is an extreme demand of time. If someone is too demanding of your time it can quickly become very wearing and usually not much that you can do will help the other person feel secure. It is important to know that if someone is too demanding of your time it can mean that they are insecure and have trust issues rather than they love you too much to be apart. In a healthy relationship people are usually able to feel completely connected but also feel completely free.

Acts of kindness

Some people are not very good at expressing their feelings verbally or physical, these people may find it easier to show love by giving acts of kindness. This could be by running a hot bath for someone to relax, making dinner or doing other tasks that make the other person's life easier or better. The problem with this is that others may not recognise this as love. These types of love can quickly become expectancies because they can get caught up in the idea that you are naturally a helpful person. If these are the things that you do to show love, the other person needs to know that this is how you feel. It is OK to tell someone that these are the things that you value and that these are the things that show love to you. Explaining your values to your partner can allow them to speak your kind of love. If acts of kindness and care are what you value most, it is necessary to be with someone who understands this. Some people can not think about others in this way and if this is what you need then your expectancies will never be met, and you will cease to be happy with your relationship.

Acknowledgment

Acknowledgement is something that is usually needed to show the other person you appreciate what they do. In abusive relationships many men who have high expectancies will not ever see any ways that you show them love. This does not give you any acknowledgment of your input and can start to become a one-sided relationship. We have seen this in the example of the spoiled perpetrator and the victim who wants to please. Without acknowledgment of your actions and efforts it can feel like you are completely ignored, that what you do does not make a difference. This is an empty kind of love, so, acknowledgment of each other's kind of efforts are extremely important.

Physical affection

Many people value physical affection in their relationship but not everybody does. If you are someone who needs physical affection it is important to be with someone who speaks this kind of love to you. While some people can become affectionate, others will never be able to express love in this way. Demanding physical affection from someone that is just not able to give it, is unhealthy for both parties in the relationship. We should not cross anyone's boundaries with the amount of affection we give or take; we need to respect each other's boundaries. The language of affection is needed but only in a respectful way to each other.

So, now I return to the questions I wrote down on deciding to date again. I promised myself I would leave if the answer to these questions were no: Would I like to see elements of this man's personality in my child, or child to be? If I was a man would I like to have this man's personality? Do I ever have to make excuses to others for this man's actions? Can I have disagreements with this man in a healthy way? Some times we can get swallowed up by an abuser, but if you have a tick list that holds things that you value in a person's personality then you may be safer from abusers.

Victims are not empty chess pieces

I feel that some notions about domestic abuse make victims feel more victimised. I would like to highlight here that as a victim you still have a place in getting in to the relationship, after all a relationship is two-way, the same as a game of chess needs two players. By this I mean that one person can not exist alone in an abusive relationship. Although we have seen that victim's identity becomes captured by their abuser, we need to acknowledge that we as victims have been brain washed by this abuser!

Referring to William Shakespeare again, he said 'all the world's a stage and all the men and women merely players.' (W., Shakespeare, 1623) There are always parts that we have that determine what happens next; we are not in this world in a one-way system. I have heard so many women say they hate that they are called a 'victim'. We do not have to be the victim if we choose not to be, but how can we do this when knowing your worth in an abusive relationship almost seems impossible? Even when you realize your worth, a lot of women stay because they believe that their partner is too dangerous to leave.

Recognising all the tactics of abuse can make it easier to understand what is happening. Know your vulnerabilities so that when someone else plays on them you are aware of what they are doing. Everyone has vulnerabilities that make us weak in some areas but knowing what they are is a strength! Knowing your faults and strengths gives you the power to be able to discard or accept negative things that any one can say about you in the future. When I was in an abusive relationship my abuser used to say that I was to hyper active and that I was like a child. For many years I hated this about myself and I stopped myself from expressing excitement, from doing silly dances and pulling funny faces. I supressed this part of my personality because I believed this was a fault in me. After my relationship ended, I was conscious about how I acted in front of others and sometimes thought about using a funny voice when telling a sorry or basically just being weird. It took many years for me to start expressing myself in this way again and when I did finally start, other people laughed, they thought my weirdness was just as funny as I thought it was! It wasn't a fault at all! Admittingly I do have faults about myself that are not great traits, but I know I have these, I don't punish myself for my faults anymore. If you truly like you, you won't care so much if others don't. I feel that getting to know yourself well may give you a better chance to hold strength in your views about who you are. This means that it will be less likely for someone abusive to start to brain wash you or change these views, or make you feel bad about them.

Task

Use your notebook to look at ideas you feel about yourself and ask yourself, are the true? In your notebook write thoughts about yourself that you have. Secondly write down at least 3 bits of evidence there are to suggest that this is true. Thirdly ask yourself was there a time when I did not think this? Look at the examples below then return to answer the questions A, B and C:

A. Negative thought I have about myself:
B. What 3 bits of evidence do I have to support this:
C. A time before I thought this:

Examples:

Person 1

A. Negative thought I have about myself:

I am nasty.

B. What 3 bits of evidence do I have to support this:

I feel nasty, my ex said I was nasty, I sometimes write nasty posts about people online.

C. A time before I thought this:

I don't know if I'm nasty because I have a lot of memories of when I have been kind.

Person 2

A. Negative thought I have about myself:

I am aggressive.

B. What 3 bits of evidence do I have to support this:

I can't control my temper, I have lashed out, I feel annoyed a

lot.

C. A time before I thought this:

I have always been quite angry, but I remember when I was

younger that I was happy.

Person 3

A. Negative thought I have about myself:

I am accepting of bad treatment.

B. What 3 bits of evidence are there to support this:

I always allow people to treat me bad, I never stick up for

myself, I am scared to stand up for myself.

C. A time before I thought this:

*I do find it hard to stand up for what I believe in because it
ends up with me being worse off, so a quiet life is better*

From these scenarios you can see that evaluating your personality can help to work out what is true and what is not true. If there are negative parts of you that you would like to change, you can! If there are parts of you that you thought were true but cannot be backed up with evidence, is this thought true? From the three people above, we look at an example of what they may have concluded from this exercise:

Person 1: I am not actually nasty I was just told I was; I am a good person; I am going to bin the idea that I am nasty.

Person 2: I do have anger issues and I would like to try and manage this part of my behaviour. I used to be happy so I know I can be happy again.

Person 3: I want to work on being more assertive and learn how to speak up for myself in a positive way. I know that when I say my opinion other people will not act like my abuser did, it is safe to say what I think.

People who have been abused in any way are usually critical of themselves. Admittedly abuse changes you; however, there are two people in a relationship, not one. You may have been the reactor living with someone who is the primary aggressor. However, if you do not change this pattern of communication you will re-enter the same pattern of relationships. It is good to acknowledge that maybe you do need to change some things about yourself, it is even better to acknowledge that your behaviours do not define you. You can separate behaviours from who you are and have new behaviours. You have everything you need to be able to control your own emotions; you have a choice and you have the power to control yourself. Some people may need extra support to realise this, such as counselling or a domestic abuse support worker or course.

Unfortunately, we cannot control others, we can't control perpetrators. But we can control ourselves and if we can do that, we stand a better chance at not being abused again. We look now at ways that negative things can just become a habit.

Changing Habits

We are creatures of habit and when we form bad habits, they can be very hard to get rid of. In fact, I feel that they are almost automatic. We learn how to do things that help us in life so that life becomes easier. I once had a driving instructor that said that I have picked up bad habits that make me a terrible driver. My instructor told me that he would rather work with a blank canvas than someone with bad habits. He said it is so much harder to unteach someone something that they now do automatically. We are supposed to keep our hands on the wheel while driving but I started to always hold the gear stick instead. My driving instructor started to tap my hand every time I took my hand off the wheel. The act of holding the gear stick happened automatically yet the constant reminder of not to do it, stopped me doing this. It took me a long time to learn how to drop this habit, but now I do not touch the gear stick and keep my hands on the wheel automatically. We spend time learning something and eventually we just do it, but it can take even more effort to unlearn it. Our brain seems to store information about a task so that we can do this with little effort in the future. I think that this basically shows that our brains want to be lazy, so it stores automatic ideas so that we don't have to think too hard.

So how can we stop ourselves doing things that just happen automatically? Much the same as my driving instructor helped me to stop touching the gear stick. If you want to stop doing something you have to unlearn it by doing repetitive things to stop. A common example I see is that you have a friend that always makes you feel worse, yet you revisit them knowing they will be a negative influence. Going over all the negative things of why you do not want to visit this friend before you visit might eventually help you to change the habit of visiting them. Maybe you visit this friend automatically.

Being in an abusive relationship is kind of like a bad habit; you learn to live it and deal with it and get used to the issues that come with it. I imagine dealing with these issues become automatic and your brain doesn't register that they are that bad anymore. Whether it's wrong treatment from a friend, an ex, or current partner, this is not OK. Do you really need this if all they bring is negativity? Maybe recognising habits this big seems impossible at this present moment, and that is OK. You can start small with changing habits, if only to show yourself that you can rewire your lazy brain. Write in your notebook the habit that you would like to change and think about how you could achieve this; you could choose any of the following options to help you:

Task

1. Visualise what it would be like to not have this habit anymore, write down positives about not doing it.
2. Look at the habit differently, focus on the positive change rather than not doing the bad habit. (think that your changing for the better and not because the habit is so bad)
3. Involve someone else that can remind you when you do the habit
4. Ask someone to change with you, share the habit change
5. Use your notebook or diary to map out days Monday to Sunday and put a tick on every day that you achieve breaking your habit
6. Put things in place that will stop you doing the habit

This chapter has focused on you as an individual, we look now at influences in the world that may affect us all in similar ways.

Chapter 5

What were our influences?

Don't believe them when they say weakness is something you

inherit!

We're not really ruined, are we?

No one is born bad; the nature versus nurture debate has supported time and time again that we are a product of our environment as well as our biological makeup. We are born good, and it is our behaviour that is sometimes bad. Weakness is not something you inherit...or is it? Why do we feel certain ways towards abuse? Why do we judge others on their experiences of abuse?

What about our historical and society influences?

Some people experience guilt after leaving their relationship especially if they have children. A lot of victims say that they crave that family unit and feel as if they have failed that they no longer have this for their child. Not so long ago it was considered unheard of to divorce. It may be innate to some of us to hold on to the idea that we have lost something important. The way that society has always described a relationship that is over is a 'failed relationship'. This wording can add to the guilt that some may feel due to a divorce or break down in relationship. We can not pretend that our grandfathers and grandmothers were not more likely to be together for life. However, in this era it was also usually the norm for women to be adaptable and for men to be the head of the household. Times have changed, and women are now seen as more equal to men. This new change does not delete the historical ideas that have been passed down to some parts of our generation. We may not recognise that our history has shaped our ideas, but societal views can give us unconscious feelings of what is seen as right, and what is wrong.

Some historical ideas are still held by older generations; however, changing times should encourage changing ideas. Not all ideas that have been passed down are relevant: we should question where our ideas come from, no matter how big or small. This would have saved me a lot of drama in the following scenario:

For years my partner and I disputed how to make a hot chocolate. My whole family always put hot chocolate mix and milk in to a pan to boil. I have been taught that this is the way to make the most delicious hot chocolate properly. My partner argued that you need to put the mix in to a microwave to make hot chocolate, and it is the better delicious outcome. This argument went on for years until one day I asked my gran: 'Why do you always put hot chocolate in a pan instead of the microwave?' My gran answered with: 'Ah, I didn't have a microwave.'

If we question why certain ideas are passed down there might be an answer as simplistic as this scenario. This is exactly why we should always question the ways we think about things and where these views have come from. Consider here your family's history pattern of relationships; how does this impact on how you view what your relationships should be like?

Task

In your notebook answer the questions below to see if any views have been passed down from your history:

1. What were your ancestors' views on women that work?
2. What were ancestors' views on not getting married or separating?
3. What were you ancestors' views about women's role in the household?

4. What were your ancestors' views on relationships in general?
5. What stories were passed on to you about the relationships that your ancestors had with each other? Stories of love and respect? Or stories of abuse?
6. What did your ancestors think about family values? Were they accepting of difference? Or would they have been ashamed?

In older generation's women would not have been able to survive alone; it was men that were able to earn the most money. Ideas of what it was like for single women back in older generations might have secretly shaped some part of our ideas today. If you have ever felt like you would not cope alone if you chose to leave your relationship, pause here and think about ways that society might have partly influenced this. Thinking about society and historical views can help you to see how the combination of this and abuse has dramatic impacts on our thoughts. Our lives are judged by others who have lived completely different lives to us, we are trying to live in a world that is changing so fast we can't keep up. Times change but some views stay the same, which means that we can not live up to the expectations of our ancestors. What else in our society gives us ideas about domestic abuse that may influence how we feel about it. We look below at other ideas.

How did we see abuse in movies?

Domestic abuse has not been taken seriously in recent history. Up until our newest generation, what men and women should be as husband and wife were viewed as private affairs. Even in old movies the ideas of abuse were promoted as 'it's just another domestic'. There have been many famous movies that portrayed reports of domestic abuse to the police as a nuisance. What message has this sent to victims that are suffering? Thankfully these ideas are far less accepted now than they ever have been. However, even today some people still overlook incidents of domestic abuse for the reasons mentioned above.

How do we see abuse in public media?

Famous singers and actors have been accused or convicted of domestic abuse on their partner. In these cases, they have lost followers overnight and their sales dropped for a short period of time. At this point some of them have chosen to make a statement explaining that they are sorry, fans then continued to support them, quickly forgetting that this person is abusive. Some may refer to that time when he slapped her, but most of the abusers did a lot more than just that. The statements of sorry are accepted and life continues, sales go back up and the abuse is looked at as much less serious than it was. Based on these ideas I ask are we seduced by famous people who say sorry, in a similar way that a victim is seduced by their abuser? If this is the case and we forgive famous people, does this not show that we all make allowances for people who abuse? This could indeed be linked back to what we explored earlier in the book with the ideas that we are given from society of what the word sorry seems to mean. Let's look now at what else society influences must answer for.

Poverty

Research has been carried out into what causal factors are common in relationships that become abusive. Poverty is considered a big factor, suggesting that there are a higher number of poor people in abusive relationships than affluent people. Statistics show that 17% of women living in the lowest income bracket experience domestic abuse, as opposed to only 4% in the highest income bracket. (Office for National statistics 2018) While poverty is noted as a causal factor of abuse, this should not stigmatise poor people who have been abused. I have worked with many other professionals that have said things along the lines of 'she will be like her mum, because they are poor, so that the cycle'. We looked in earlier chapters at children who are likely to fall in to the cycle of abuse, are those who have grown up in abusive homes. However abusive homes and poverty-stricken homes still can produce children who become scholars. If we receive the right support, we can break free from these cycles and change our future for the better. I know this to be true because in the years I have worked with domestic abuse, I have witnessed change in people who accepted support.

Culture

Domestic abuse has also been found to be higher in different cultures. This is said to be due to some cultural beliefs that view men are top of the hierarchy. Some countries have traditional norms that view men as superior to women. Females are not supported to receive education and recent attacks on women who engage in education have included acid attacks to their face. Female genital mutilation is accepted in some nations as a cultural norm; this is to ensure that women do not have pleasure from sexual acts or due to religious beliefs, ideas of cleanliness or societal views. This type of abuse is normalised in these cultures; it is the history that is still prevalent in their society today. It is difficult to change something that is accepted in a whole society. Looking at the power of society it can be difficult to understand how a whole nation of people can follow morals that others may find ethically wrong. How can people follow lifestyles such as this if others see that it is morally wrong? When there is a shared idea amongst a society it can be difficult to show them otherwise. Everybody has a purpose and if that same purpose is shared with others, this is confirmation that it is more right, that it is OK, and for the good of them as a collective.

This chapter has looked at influences that may have come from society. While weakness is not something you inherit, it seems that some ideas that we are passed on may give us weaknesses in how we cope with our lives today. Right, now we know that, let's move on!

<u>What are my needs?</u>

To work out your own personality traits and where these might have come from, use your notebook and answer the following questions. Can you link any behaviours that you currently have that may be linked to the way you were brought up?

<u>Task</u>

> 1. Think about your childhood and how you felt your needs were met; were you listened to? Were you listened to too much and not challenged? How comfortable do you feel today with expressing what you think?

2. Who was your biggest influence in life? Was this good or bad? Are they still an influence?

3. Could you express your feelings? Do you express you're feeling well today? Did you have a good social group in school? If not, why? Can you develop friends well today?

4. Were you able to say when you were upset? How was this dealt with? Do you mask your real upset emotions to suit other people? Or do you make your emotions known?

5. Did you feel part of the family or were you on the outside? Do you feel part of groups now in your adult life?

6. Did you feel safe as a child? What are your ideas of dangerous situations? Do you feel unsafe in any areas of life today?

7. Do you remember being bullied at school? Did the teacher ever tell you to say sorry and you thought it was unfair? Did the teachers ever help in a way you thought

> was helpful? Have there been many other times in your life like this?

Looking at these questions may help you to work out why you think and feel certain ways today. As noted previously, understanding emotions after an abusive relationship can be very difficult. I have recognised that anger and upset can be unstable in many women who experience abuse. We look now at the regulation of these two emotions after experiences of abuse.

Anger as a reaction emotion

Feeling angry for no reason can be a sign that there is something going on that you are not aware of. Having a much angrier reaction than you should to a small issue can also be a sign that there is something else happening here.

If you feel like you are naturally an angry person, why is this? Could it be that in fact you are anxious, upset or scared about your safety, feelings or wellbeing? If you have always felt wrongly judged by your partner, this would mean that you are constantly in defence mode. To protect yourself you might have the attitude that: if my anger is bigger than yours, you will leave me alone. To describe this in simple terms is, it's like a tiny monkey squaring up to the gorillas by standing up puffing his chest out. Or the snake that rises to show height over other animals. We're not that different to animals and sometimes we feel small. It is when we feel small and vulnerable that we might use anger to hide this feeling.

Being angry gives the impression we are strong and that we are confident. If you can relate to this type of anger, what are you fearful of? Is there something that can help you to feel safer or more valued? Feeling anger towards people who have not wronged you can often mean that the anger is masked by other emotions, which could be upset, jealousy, fear or insecurity. This feeling can be difficult to accept because jealousy or insecurity are thought to be undesired traits. But these are normal human feelings we have; if you push these feelings aside and ignore them it is likely that anger will seep out. It's a competitive world out there and sometimes we can have strong feelings of dislike towards others that have not wronged us, but we are angry because we would like to be like they are or have what they have. So many times, in my life I have seen a group of women criticise and belittle the most beautiful girl in the bar at a night club. What this achieves is ... nothing; it does not make you any more beautiful and it does not make her less beautiful.

How you criticise people will not improve you; it will only make you feel worse. If you feel strong dislike for someone that has not caused you any wrong, or you are judgmental of their actions, try and evaluate what you really feel. I really do believe that this is the first step to overcoming feeling negative about yourself. Believe in yourself and your strengths; if you are not able to show love for yourself then you may be drawn to being negative and critical about others. This can be a refreshing idea when we think of how others treat us. Others only outwardly treat us badly when they feel bad in themselves. In future if someone wrongs you, do not ask the question: what is wrong with me that they have done this? Instead ask the question: what is wrong with them for them to have done this? When you reverse this question, you stop looking for what is wrong with you and instead realise it is them.

Upset as a reaction emotion

Upset is a normal reaction to have if you have been wronged. This can happen for many reasons, one possibly being that people have different ways they rate their self-worth. A person who holds the view that you need to text back quickly in order to show you care may be really upset when they do not receive a quick text back. What is going on here? Why does this person think that they are unwanted or uncared for if they don't receive that quick text? This person does not consider rational thoughts about why others haven't text back, which could be a sign that this upset is a reaction emotion that is masking another hidden emotion.

You cannot control others, nor can you expect that they should drop everything to do what you want. If someone does not find it important to respond quickly to texts, they may not recognise that this is important to others. We sometimes make sure that we treat others the way we would like to be treated, but they may not recognise what you do if they do not share the same values and importance's as you. Here we see that feeling upset can be due to the expectancy that others should meet our expectancies. It might be useful to pause here and think of your own expectancies of others and how you feel when others do not meet your expectancies. Do others have different expectancies to you? Do you have high expectancies of what others should be doing for you? Or are other people's expectations too high for you to meet?

What if you feel like you have no control over your reaction emotions, and you think that these are your real emotions. I work with many clients who experience anger issues, their anger reactions are often way too severe for the issue that has arisen. I can think of an example where one of my friends had experienced a chaotic few months but had coped well with it all and did not complain at all. However, one day she ran out of tomato sauce and she threw the bottle on the floor in a temper, swore and shouted extremely loud then fell to her knees and cried. We can all surely recognise that she wasn't this upset about sauce, right? Emotions are not productive or healthy when used in this way, however I do recognise when you are in this state of mind it is difficult to control it, especially if you haven't connected your emotions to the underlying issue. For my friend it was all the chaotic things that had happened in the month, the empty sauce allowed her to release these emotions.

You can't just stop emotions

After an abusive relationship it can be hard to feel anything at all let alone understand how to express emotions. Many clients look to me and say, if I am angry, I am just angry, and I can't stop that. This is true, when you feel something you can't stop the feeling from arising, but you can choose how you behave with this feeling. Some days I choose to swear at the man who cuts me up on the motorway and other days I choose not to. I have that choice – it is me who swears, and it is me who ignores him.

Regulating your emotions can be hard when you feel like you have no control over them. You can learn to express your emotions in a healthy way that is not destructive to you or others. If you feel sad you must get that out, but in a healthy way. If you feel angry, you must get that out, but in a healthy way. Talking about how you feel can help to put things in to perspective.

Unfortunately, we aren't all fined tuned in to understanding how best to regulate our emotions. We are all walking around with our own answers but fail to be able to reach them most of the time. If you imagine that your feelings are a fizzy liquid in an airtight bottle.

Every time you feel sad or angry this bottle is getting more and more full. Over time there is way too much liquid and the liquid in the bottle has no alternative than to hiss out. This hissing liquid comes out fast and happens in a destructive way because there is no control over it. We need to learn to open the bottle to tip our feelings out slowly, and not let so much pressure build up. I am not suggesting that you are a super human and should never feel angry or upset again, this is not what regulation is about. It is a way of realising negative emotions that need to be addressed appropriately. You can get trapped in the pattern of how you regulate your emotions. What barriers do you have in expressing your emotions? Are there ways that you can get feelings out without it being destructive?

Sometimes it feels like learned behaviours cannot be changed, but they can. If I said to you, think of a coffee shop, you can easily pull on ideas in your head that you have about a coffee shop. Maybe the smell of the coffee, the type of cup they have, how you make an order, the staff's uniform, cakes and other ideas about your past experiences. But what if I said to you were going to a coffee shop that doesn't sell coffee. You would question why? Why are they called a coffee shop? We question things that aren't normal to us and just accept the things that are. We have built connected patterns of ideas about what is normal to us and we don't even think about them anymore, they are the norm. I feel that your emotions just happen automatically, just like you automatically have ideas about what a coffee shop is. I encourage you to always question why you feel like you do? Let's start by tacking your emotions throughout you week.

Task

Use your notebook to track emotions that you feel that may be too severe for the event, start by answering the questions here:

1. Write down the event that happened to make you feel like you did.
2. Write down your negative emotion when you feel it, what is this emotion? How strong was it? What did you do when you felt this? What did it feel like in your body?
3. Do your emotions match the event or were they to severe for the issues? (Sometimes past emotions are attached to our current emotions which make us overreact to the problem)

See the examples below to understand what possible reaction emotions can be.

Reaction Emotion: I shouted at a work colleague because she didn't help me use the printer.

Possible feeling: I was always told by my abuser that I am stupid. I couldn't work the printer and felt stupid, so I got angry to cover the fact I couldn't use it to avoid feeling stupid.

Reaction emotion: My grandad called and said he would be late to pick me up, I shouted at him and told him not to bother coming to get me at all.

Possible feeling: My grandad has always let me down in important situations, so this felt like it was the final straw.

Take time to evaluate your negative emotions throughout the day, what have you over reacted to and why. We might exaggerate our experiences which can sometimes fool you in to feeling much worse than you need to about a current event. This can also be opposing when we minimise an event, so we say that it wasn't as bad as it was. We look now at how me minimise.

Minimising

Many family members of victims do not understand why victims of abuse minimise in certain situations. Some victims have said they were asked questions like; 'why did you lie', or 'why didn't you say what happened'. Some of the reasons I have been told by victims are listed here:

- Some victims do not recognise abuse because they accept a certain level of bad treatment as normal. Therefore, when they minimise the abuse, they may honestly feel it's not that bad.

- People tend to compare their abuse to the worst-cases possible, which can leave them feeling like their abuse is not that bad.

- Some abused women are scared to tell anyone about how bad their abuse is out of fear that, if they do, the abuser will harm them.

- When you are in an abusive relationship your partner may often minimise what they have done to you: 'it was only a tap'. This stops recognition of the severity of the abuse and can make you feel that it's OK.

It is important to acknowledge how bad your abuse was, but this can be done in your own time. Some people still minimise their abuse because they are still scared, others do it because this keeps them safe from feeling too sad about what's happened.

Task

Write down in your note pad the answers to these questions:

1. What have you minimised before that you now know was worse than how you saw it to be?
2. Do you know that all the types of abuse that we have covered so far are never acceptable behaviours?
3. If you remember something upsetting or horrific do you laugh, or have you laughed when telling the story?
3. Is there part of you that recognises that this was not funny?

> 4. Do you need extra help to connect with these feelings, such as counselling?

Sometimes humour makes it easier to deal with negative emotions, and this can be very useful for dealing with heavy issues. To speak seriously about things that hurt can take courage, and not everyone will be ready to talk about their experiences straight away. Talking about things can only happen when you feel ready to do so, counselling does not work if you do not want to engage in it.

Know that:

- Realising that you are worthy enough to be heard can take time

- There are people that will want to listen to how you feel

- Being able to choose the right people to open up to will take practice

- You have a voice that is just as valid as anybody else

- You are important

We explore the next chapter to look at the different ways in which some of us might choose to negatively cope with our abuse.

chapter 6

How do you cope?

If you can change, then so can I

<u>What do you use to cope?</u>

Let's take the time through this chapter to look at h we cope in today's world. Many victims of abuse express their pain in negative ways because the emotion is sometimes too much to tolerate. I have witnessed many victims become obsessive with different coping mechanisms. Some are obsessed with sports, cleaning, controlling plans or have obsessive thoughts. This seems to be manageable for most women and they explain that they need to have some level of control over their life so that they feel ok. I have worked with many women who go as far as saying they hate surprises because they need to be in control of what is ahead of them. There are others who develop negative coping skills and it is here that they become harder to manage.

I have noted below the negative coping mechanisms that I have witnessed in victims that I have worked with and the ways in which they use them.

<u>Self-harm</u>

Self-harm is a negative coping mechanism, which is used by many people who experience abuse. Like many other bad coping mechanisms, self-harm causes the feeling of adrenaline. The addiction can become physical, much like the addiction to drama that was explained in an earlier chapter. Self-harm can include cutting yourself, skin picking, squeezing yourself or any behaviour that purposely inflicts harm on yourself. Talking to someone about self-harm is always a good idea, sharing issues with others can make you work out your feelings, stop self-harming and make you safer. Over the last 6 years of my counselling profession I have noticed the following 3 patterns (which are my observations not fact) in people that self-harm, they may fit with you if you have ever self-harmed:

Pattern 1.

High stress levels

Unable to cope with stress

Final stress trigger

Self-harm

Relief and control

This form of self-harm is triggered from the inability to cope with stressful situations. This can sometimes be from not being able to express yourself or living in a high state of stress in an abusive relationship. Meditation and mindfulness practices have worked best with this form of self-harm. (These practices are looked at in more depth in later chapters).

Pattern 2.

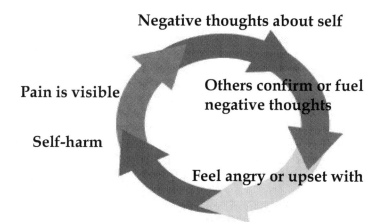

I have found Pattern 2 in people who hold many negative views about themselves. When others confirm or fuel these thoughts, anger and upset with others arise. Being unable to verbally discuss feelings with others causes the need to self-harm. Many clients have said they like this as their pain becomes visible to them and others. In some cases, I have seen this form of self-harm is associated with having a poor image of self, therefore when others impact your wellbeing in any way it can cause you to spiral. Positive affirmations and work on self-worth tend to work well with this form of self-harm. (This practice is looked at in more depth in later chapters).

Pattern 3.

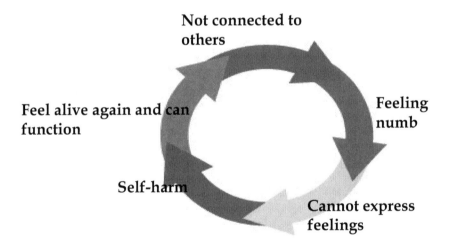

Pattern 3 shows a more dissociative type of issue, where you feel that you cannot connect with others. This leaves you feeling numb; you feel misunderstood and alone at this stage. It is difficult to express feelings when you do not feel connected to anyone and this then leads to self-harm to release feelings. Some that fit in this pattern have said that self-harm is carried out with hatred for the self or feeling unworthy of others attention. I have found that this form of self-harm is usually hidden from others.

To overcome this addiction is difficult, if you have never learned to express your emotions to others, self-harm may seem like the only way to get your feelings out. As previously noted, exercising can help to alleviate the physical need to self-harm due to the chemical releases that your body is craving. Planning your own safety is crucial if you are addicted to self-harming; the following ideas could help to keep you safe:

Task

- Write one message on 5 different pieces of paper as to why you shouldn't self-harm. Wrap what you use to self-harm in the paper and stick them down. Read each one before you choose to use this item again. (This can help you to see that self-harm is not the answer.)

• Track your mood throughout the day to try and evaluate what went wrong and why you feel like you want to self-harm
• Question yourself: is this to get back at others? Is this because you are angry or upset? Will this help in any way to achieve what I want? Will this stop what is making me sad?
• Make your own safety plan by removing any items from your surroundings that you would use to self-harm
• Tell someone that you self-harm
• Talk to someone if you feel like self-harming; this can be through helplines, agencies, your doctor, family or friends
• Mediation/mindfulness
• Understand how your negative thoughts make you feel

Alcohol and drugs

Some people choose to use alcohol or drugs to block their emotions; unfortunately, this dependency then becomes the problem. Before working out who you are it is important to know who you are not. 'I am an alcoholic' or 'I am a drug taker' encompasses who you are and becomes your identity. It is almost expected that some teenagers will experiment with drugs and alcohol. This type of drug and alcohol use may not ever lead to an addiction. For young people who are experiencing abuse, drug and alcohol use maybe used to mask negative emotions, here is where the use can be dissociative and destructive. Experimenting with drugs can quickly become a coping mechanism for people experiencing or witnessing abuse at home. Drugs and alcohol may become your social norm, which is expected to happen amongst friends. During this period in life it is important to be aware of your mood when you are not influenced by drugs and alcohol. If you notice shifts in priorities, mood, behaviour, social interactions, these could all be signs that you are developing an addiction.

The dependency to drugs and alcohol is progressive and can end in fatality. Not everyone becomes addicted to drugs. People have overcome these addictions before and will continue to overcome these issues in the future. This gives hope that anyone can overcome an addiction, it is important to work hard at losing this as an identity so that you can learn who you really are.

People may choose to self-medicate with alcohol and drugs to drown out feelings of being alone, worthlessness, loss or upset. Alcohol and drugs can mask what you can achieve and what you are actually capable of. 'I have a few glasses of red wine at night' sounds more acceptable; however, if this is a dependency that you can't function without, I put it to you that this is in the category of a bad coping mechanism. If you have a severe addiction, it's always important to consult a doctor or alcohol support worker before you choose to change. There is support out there for this if you use this as a coping mechanism. While 'I am an alcoholic' or 'I am a drug taker' exist as an identity, it will stop you from reaching your abilities to become something more.

Eating disorders

Eating disorders have been associated with negative coping strategies of domestic abuse. I have worked with many women who say they did not eat because their abuser said they were fat. I have worked with many others that said they binged to deal with the emotional stress of their abuse. Again, these coping mechanisms seem to be physical as well as psychological. There are many different types of eating disorders but here I look at binge eating and anorexia as these are the two issues that I have worked with most.

Anorexia

I have been told many different reasons why become anorexic, clients have said that:

- They genuinely think they are fat
- They feel like they don't deserve food
- They feel that it is the only thing they control
- They think they look better this way
- They can't stop calorie counting and not eating is like a game where they want to see if they can eat as little as possible for as long as possible.

Like most other issues that we have looked at so far, anorexia effects your body as well as your mind. Your body starts to eat itself when you do not eat, this can bring around a feeling of euphoria. This issue may have started with fasting, or feeling weight was becoming an issue. It is hard to recognise weight loss if you always see yourself as a fat person in your head. During domestic abuse an abuser might tell their partner that they are fat, and this then becomes engrained in their heads and it's difficult for them to recognise their own body as thin or healthy. Some have said that they have low self-worth and do not feel worthy of food. I have been told that these people enjoy cooking big meals for others but will not themselves touch the food. I have worked with some people that calorie count which they say causes them to become obsessive with numbers: how many days can I go without food? how many calories did I have? This is an obsessive behaviour and you may need to seek medical advice if you can not break the cycle of anorexia.

Binge eating

People who have binge eating disorder have said that they feel judged and that their disorder is not considered a major thing compared to anorexia. However, from binge eating they suffer from physical conditions such as diabetes and, in severe cases, heart attacks.

Clients have told me that binge eating disorder is obsessive and brings intrusive thoughts that arise every day. Unfortunately, I have been told that when clients experience a binge, they may choose to starve themselves the following morning. Going without breakfast the day after a binge seems to be one of the worst thing you can do as your body then craves even more sugar dense foods throughout the day. It seems that when you starve your body it quickly starts to burn up energy and you instantly crave more high-energy food such as carbohydrates.

Binge eating is not only due to hunger and craving carbohydrates; women have said it can be caused by emotional upset, stress, comments made by others that you disagree with, tiredness, loneliness, boredom or just that it is a habit. Overcoming binge eating is a mindset, it is learning self-control, knowing your triggers and putting safety planning in place for when you feel like you are going to binge.

What's the same in coping mechanisms?

All the above have one common factor which is: if you learn self-control and self-regulation you can more effectively overcome these issues. This entire book focuses on learning self-control, and self-regulation starting with small tasks. Overcoming small things can enable you to overcome the bigger things. Often our addictions and obsessions can be connected to our past experiences, some women have suggested that their addiction can be the effect of an exact event that happened to them during their abuse. We look now at ways that we may revisit our past.

Why am I still drawn to my past?

As humans we are quite sentimental; we need to share meaning and be understood by others. We need to place meanings on situations so that we can process it and move forward with our lives. Not being able to let go of the past is the route problem for most victims of abuse. Most people think that if your past is in your head, you can easily choose to just not think about it.

My friend read a quote out to me not so long ago which read: 'Do not live in the past, there is nothing there for you'. But what if there is? What if you need to revisit the past to make sense of what happened? What if it all happened too quick for you to process? What if we revisit our past because we were not in our right mind at the time, and we need to look back with clearer vision. What if we need to revisit the past to make sense of what happened to us?

When you experience domestic abuse, you just go through it; the breaking up and making up happens fast. You don't really have much time to process the breaking-up phase because, before you know it, you are back in the making-up phase again. When you are being controlled and manipulated you don't have time to fully recognise what has happened, never mind how you feel about it. After experiences of abuse it just makes sense that you revisit the past to work out how you feel about what you experienced. Our feelings can spring us back in to our past; sometimes we don't want to revisit, but our feelings make our minds go down memory lane.

Let's take a look now at what feelings may take us back to our past and why.

Revisiting past through upset

You may revisit the past through upset feelings. This might be that you keep revisiting the things you did that were taken for granted – revisiting incidents that have emotionally scarred you yet have not affected your ex-partner at all. You may revisit the past because it is upsetting to acknowledge that your ex-partner can just move on after ruining your life. If someone is expectant, they will never see what you have done for them. In their eyes they deserve it all, and if you don't comply, you're in the wrong it is always your fault.

You may be searching in the past for answers of why and how they would do this to you. But the answer is that they can't do anything else because until they learn that others are just as worthy as them, they just can't acknowledge other's feelings. You can't expect someone to do a test in the Polish language if they only speak French. The same as you can't expect someone to appreciate you if they have never appreciated anything. Revisiting the past is OK; you may need to be upset about what has happened to you. Pushing upsetting memories out of your mind may make it more difficult to move forward. We look at techniques later in the book for trying to control upsetting memories.

Revisiting the past through anger

We might revisit the past in anger. You may be angry that you have been treated badly by your ex-partner. It is OK to feel angry about it; you *should* feel angry about it. Anger should be visited but not lived in. As hard as it is you need to let go of anger for your own sake. Anger is not productive in changing anything for you; you are angry, and this is only affecting you. It isn't fair that this has happened to you. It shouldn't have happened. Anger can come with the disbelief that this person has treated you like this. Women I have worked with tend to say that the anger they feel is due to the unfairness that they feel about what they have been through. I have worked with women who have overcome their anger by accepting that the person that broke them was also broken. Too broken for them to fix. This does not make it right, but it can help make sense of it. When you process that this person was broken it can draw some people back to feeling sorry for them but no matter what you did, they wouldn't have changed. Sometimes you need to let fires burn, because trying to put them out will only engulf you in!

Revisiting the past through guilt

Some victims still hold severe amounts of guilt about the breakdown of their relationship. This guilt pulls them back to their past to go over what they feel they have done wrong. Perpetrators have the ability to make you feel that what they did, was somehow, your fault. The perpetrator may have played the victim role. This would have been where they share their story of their horrible upbringing, horrible addictions, or horrible friends. When victims know the perpetrator's unfortunate life story, they can't help but be drawn back to memories, due to guilt. Victims feel guilty because they felt they were the only one who ever really cared about this person. The guilt that it didn't work, the guilt that you didn't succeed in helping this person. The truth is, you could not have saved this person from themselves, they made you believe that you could stop them from being who they were. That you brought out a side in them that was nice, but this does not mean that you could have helped them get rid of the bad parts of who they are. It is never your responsibility to make someone a better person, they need to do this on their own.

You deserve someone who is already a good person. You can spend, days, weeks, months and sometimes years trying to put pieces of someone else together or you can just leave all the pieces on the floor and move on.

Intrusive revisits to the past caused by fear

You may have no control over revisiting your past. Maybe your memories just pop up even though you don't want them to. In this instance you can fear your past; you fear it because you still have no control over it. Maybe memories are too scary to think about and you feel that you need to stop thinking about them straight away. This can make them worse and make them occur more. If your fear is for your safety, there are things that can be done to help you feel safer. Sometimes feeling safer can stop intrusive thoughts that happen out of fear. Triggers that remind you of past events can mean that you still do not feel safe. Are there ways you can implement more safety measures? Check the back pages of this book for more advice about safety measures that may help you.

You might know your fear is not rational and you are unlikely to be in actual danger. If this is the case, you may have an argument in your head of irrational and rational thoughts. Your irrational though might be:

'I heard a noise upstairs; it could be him.'

Your rational thought, however, might immediately argue back with:

'He doesn't even know where you live.'

This type of argument is one that we all have in many different situations of our lives. Once you become aware of this argument, you can try to make your rational thought the stronger thoughts. You could go over four or five rational thoughts before jumping back to an irrational one. You do not have to be scared about your past; do not be scared to revisit it you are OK now.

Searching for meaning in the past

Sometimes it is just unbelievable that someone would treat you this badly. Maybe you search through memories to look for more reasons, something you have missed in the past. Something that shows why he did this, why it happened. People do horrific things to one another and sometimes it just doesn't make any sense. We give ourselves too much credit because when we look at the horrific things, we do to each other, we are no better than animals in clothes. Sometimes people are just less emotionally developed than others and their ability to understand other's emotions are impossible. In my opinion these are the unlucky ones, not us as victims. Because despite the amount of pain these abusers cause others, they may never fully connect with others to feel at peace with themselves.

We think that we operate on a higher level of being and sometimes we look for meanings that don't exist. Sometimes people are underdeveloped emotionally, socially and psychologically, which means they operate from a lesser level than others. So, the answers you search for of why this happened, may just be that they did not have the capability to act any other way.

Whatever reason you are visiting your past, take from it what you need and leave!

Chapter 7

Will I ever feel connected again?

That's when I knew my invisible friend had become too big to

keep

Why don't I view others like I did?

Pushing others away can be a form of coping after experiencing domestic abuse. This can be for any of the following reasons:

- Because you do not trust others have your best interests at heart

- You cannot cope with judgement or questions about the abuse

- You cannot pretend to be the person you were before the abuse

- You can not bare that someone may ask, 'Are you OK?'

- You feel to confused to be part of a conversation and can't process what people say

These feelings come with the after-effects of domestic abuse, but this does not mean this will be forever. I have found that, much like the grief of a death happens in stages, so does the reality of leaving a domestically abusive relationship:

Stage 1: **Shock:** You leave the relationship and are in a state of shock. At this stage you cannot think about the past, present or future and are confused about what has happened. There is a numbness with limited amounts of feelings about what has happened.

Stage 2: **Unawareness/denial:** You are unaware of how dangerous your partner was for you. You do not recognise the impacts that they had on you nor do you recognise all the abusive behaviours that were distributed. You minimise your abuse as they may have always told you it was your fault. You acknowledge your part in causing the abusive behaviour, you do not feel like you were in danger. You think that he acted out of love, not jealousy or controlling behaviours.

Stage 3: **Awareness:** You begin to process some of your experiences and see that it was a toxic and dangerous relationship. You acknowledge that he may never have loved you and is a textbook perpetrator or just incapable of putting others before himself. You may start to acknowledge that the abuse was not our fault.

Stage 4: **Possible return to stage 2**: It is possible that stage 2 and 3 will be revisited in a cycle of denial and awareness. This can be because it is difficult to acknowledge that a partner may not have cared or loved you. It can also be difficult to accept that it was not your fault due to being told throughout the relationship that it was.

Stage 5: **Upset/Anger:** You are upset and angry about the abuse; you question how and why someone could do this. In this stage you may start to think about the other person more. As noted above unanswered questions may become more difficult to deal with, such as: 'why would he do this?'; 'how can he just move on when my life feels ruined?'

Stage 6: **Acceptance**: You begin to accept what has happened and understand what domestic abuse is. You begin to recognise patterns of abusive behaviour and start to make sense of your abuse.

Stage 7: **Becoming able**: You start to learn how to live again, make small achievements and take small steps towards becoming independent again.

There are no set time frames for these stages; you could stay in either stage for any period. If you have the correct support, it could help you to get through these stages quicker. Some women that have got to stage 2 only a few days after fleeing from their partner. You may feel like you are at the end stage and then slip back, but this does not mean the progress you have made has gone, you still have managed to get to the end stage. Choosing to talk to a family member or friend may not be the best option if you feel that they would not understand, doing this can make things feel worse. In this case try and use other people to talk to so that you can get the right support. Talking helps you to process what you have been through and can help to give you a better perspective on what has happened. Let's now complete the task here, to evaluate what stage you are currently in.

Task 7

In your notebook write down the answers to the following questions:

1.What stage do you feel you are in?

2. What realisations or thoughts are you having at the stage?
3. What ideas are you struggling with that may be stopping you from getting to the next stage?
4. How could you process your experiences and thoughts to move forward to the next stage?

It has been suggested in this chapter that talking is important, but for some women it is difficult to be able to be around others let alone open up to them. We look now at ways that can make it easier to connect with others and why we might be struggling with this.

Connecting with others

After experiencing abuse, it can be hard to connect with others, even in small talk. It is natural as humans to be anxious creatures. If you imagine what it would have been like to live in tribes years ago, we would have had our own communities. The closest communities may have been way too far away to have ever met each other. We would have lived in our tribe and got used to who we see every day. We would have needed a level of anxiety if we saw a stranger, because that could mean that there were intruders that could be dangerous. Currently in the world we live in we have had to adapt to strangers everywhere. If living with people we know is our natural inbuilt system due to our heritage as humans, it is no wonder why we sometimes feel anxious when we are in a food store around strangers!

It is in our makeup to be controlled in a system so that the world can work in less chaos. It is in our makeup to live with anxiety so that we could have survived years ago. If we did not have anxiety, we would be much less cautious, we wouldn't look when we cross the road, we wouldn't care about getting hurt. So here we see that it is innate for us to have anxiety. But also, it is necessary to have anxiety so that we can be safe, we judge situations and people every day to keep ourselves physically and emotionally safe. So, we are constantly judging people around us to make sure that they are good people that will not hurt us in anyway. During an abusive relationship this sense that we have seems to get heightened and then we are always searching for danger in others. This can make it difficult to be out amongst many people.

Connecting in honesty

I hear most victims of abuse say that they cannot answer people truthfully when they're asked, 'How are you?' Or that they can only socialise for a short amount of time because they can't keep up pretending to be happy. We are social beings and whether we like it or not we need each other's company to feel OK. We do also need alone time, but if we need to be alone because being with people is painful then we are in a nasty cycle. Being with people makes us feel bad, so we need to be alone, but being alone then makes us feel lonely so we need to be around people. The reason you may not feel connected to people can be understood from the most basic point of view. To have a meaningful relationship of any kind I suggest that there needs to be a level of honesty. This honesty needs to be present in your feelings towards each other, the reciprocated conversations need to be real. After domestic abuse you might not even know who you are, so how can you be able to act authentically with others.

There needs to be this basic connection of: I understand how you feel, and you understand how I feel so that we can relax in someone's company. Without this base level of authenticity, true relational depth is almost impossible. Being honest about how you feel can help you connect with others and allow others to truly connect with you.

If you have close family members or friends that do not quite understand how you feel and it is difficult for you to be honest with them, you could write a letter to them explaining how you feel. Writing letters is a good way to start letting other people know what you are feeling. Being honest about how you feel can help you to connect with people; it's OK to tell someone, 'I actually have no idea how I feel.' It's also OK to tell someone, 'I'm really not good at socialising right now because I feel …' We all understand what it is to feel nervous, down, scared or confused so there will be a level of understanding from others. Sometimes the act of voicing to someone that you feel anxious/sad/scared/angry can stop you feeling this because it brings it out into the open. It is not something that you have to conceal while conversing with someone. We have so far looked at judging the safety of others and having an honest relationship so that you can be open. Now we look at the physical side of connecting with others and how this can impact on your feelings.

Connecting with physical contact

For women who have been physically abused, affection in the form of touch can be difficult. Women say that they push family members away or repeat the word no when they try and hug them. Others say that they can not cry in front of people out of fear they may offer affection.

- some feel that if they are shown contact, they will not be able to stop crying. This is OK, crying is not a vulnerability; it is OK to cry, and maybe you need to. This can be difficult to do, but if someone is offering affection, they are opening the door for you to cry it out to them.

- Some hold blame and guilt too close to be able to find themselves worthy of affection from others. Some victims feel that they have acted wrongly and can not accept affection from others because they do not feel that they deserve it.

- Some have said that they cannot be touched because they have associated touch with their negative experiences.

- Some have said they are unsure of why they can no longer accept affection. I recall that the people that have said this have mostly had partners that were not very receptive to affection.

Some abusers respond to affection with verbal or physical abuse which might mean that they are incapable of giving affection. Other abusers refuse affection from their partner and deny them any physical signs of love at all. This may have made you associate affection with abuse, and this may well be the reason why you find it difficult to give affection now. If you are someone who cannot bear to receive affection from others at this time, I ask you to be kind to yourself. You may not be able to accept others' touch, but can you accept your own? This is a good place to start; this is a good place to start even if you have not experienced physical or sexual abuse. When you feel alone or upset or vulnerable, give yourself a hug and tell yourself it is OK. Really feel your arms in your hands and tell yourself that you are loved. This might seem like a bizarre request but to be able to receive love from others, you first may need to be OK with yourself.

It is OK to have boundaries, if you know what they are you know what you accept and what you don't. Some women like to have control again over the people who can touch them, this control may be exercised until they feel strong enough to embrace others or be embraced. A lot of victims I have worked with get extremely upset with how their friends or family have reacted to their experiences of abuse. They have said that this pushes them further away from people and they get hurt easily by others. This then stops them from wanting to give physical affection to others because they fear that they can not trust them. It is important to recognise that sometimes, people who truly love you, do get things wrong.

When people get it wrong

How many times have you heard a sentence that starts with 'no offence'? We all know that this sentence usually ends with the most offensive thing that someone can say about you. Here in communication we excuse what we say by using words that state we don't mean it. Why say it then? If you have to say that you don't mean offence, can you at least explain why you think it is not offensive? Where are you coming from if you do not come from a place of offence? Words that people use can come out wrong and it is your right to ask what they mean by this. You are owed the right to ask someone to expand on what they mean, and this can be done without conflict. There are times that you have needed to stick up for yourself, and maybe did not do this for your own safety. Or maybe you have become used to meeting offensive words with retaliating offensive words. This might be your style of communicating now, but does this ever get the point across? If you shout louder or say something worse, does this really achieve anything? When we end up in this style of communication our opinions and feelings are not acknowledged, they are not heard. Sometimes no matter how you communicate with someone they will never actually acknowledge either of these things. This may be because they do not have the ability to see things through our eyes. Having the last word just does not matter if the person you are talking at is incapable of understanding.

After domestic abuse you can be very sensitive to other's opinions; I imagine that you are to hurt to accept any more negatives. You have been through a unique experience and most people do not fully know the impact of it. Unfortunately, this means that they may not give the best reactions, and this can sometimes feel insensitive or judgmental. This may not be their fault; you cannot expect people to know how you feel or understand your experience, but you can tell them about it. Show them this book if you feel like it will help; people that want to know how you feel will want to learn about the impacts of abuse.

When you are a victim of abuse you can feel like a victim of other things. Many women, including me, have fallen in to this trap. We look for ways that others might sabotage us, belittle us or become paranoid about other's intentions. We naturally slip in to feeling like a victim because we have been there for so long before!

We have been victims of abuse, but we do not have to be victims of anything else. We have the power to converse how we want, voice our opinions as we want and to achieve what we want.

Can you feel connected with others without connecting?

Connection can be something that you feel, and maybe face to face connection is just too much to think about right now. To work towards being connected with others it might be useful to start on a more distant level. I realise this sounds opposing: how can we be distant but connected? Let's explore this idea.

After having my son, I split up with his farther and became a single mother. I was single for about three years. Anyone who knows what it is like to be a single mum will know that at your children's bedtime, you are housebound. I spent most evenings reading, reading about everything and anything. I was interested in anything that involved human interactions, from topics that included quantum physics, art, witchcraft, music, psychology, counselling, sports and religion. I began to obsess about similarities between us as humans; we have so many differences, but what is the same? The understanding that I am the same in ways as others brought strong feelings of connectedness. I began to feel part of something bigger, and all past traumas seemed to feel less painful. I am an abuse victim, but I am also human so what parts of who I am are the same as other humans? I needed to know these answers so that I could still feel human, so that I could still feel like I am OK, and I belong in this world. I started trying to understand different religions and their ideas about how we are supposed to live. I couldn't put myself in any one religious' category, so I looked for similarities that existed through all of them.

Religions hold different beliefs that separate one group from another, but there are some concepts that are shared among many religions. Religious beliefs cannot be proven as fact, but the most shared ideas, to me, hold more weight. What shared ideas am I talking about? Why am I even talking about religion in a book about abuse? The thing is, although I am not religious I feel that scriptures are a good guideline of how to live. Most scriptures give us a good idea of morals and how we can live as happy humans. It is hard to find a life guide of how to be if you have never really had any good influences in life, but this is what I felt I found while reading different religious books. One thing that helped me to feel better towards others was truly believing that we are all connected in some way. We share the same biological make up, we are the same species, we can understand each other more than we are able to understand any other species on the planet. You may feel alone in your experience, but there will have been millions of people that have walked on this earth that have experienced things in the same way you have. The people around you may not understand the impact of your abuse but there are thousands of women who do! You are not alone in your experience if you think about it in this way. We are part of an era of change, more and more people are acknowledging the impact of abuse. To explain why I came to the idea that we are all the same and connected as humans I now share some of my findings that made me think this. For those who do not want to read about religion or think they can not share religious beliefs feel free to skip to the next chapter. However, the next few paragraphs explain the way that I changed how I viewed myself following my abusive relationship. The following concepts are not about religion or science as such, its more about the wider picture that we are all human.

We are all one

There are many passages in religious scriptures and teachings that suggest that we are all connected as one. The Christian bible reads: 'so we, though many, are one body in Christ, and individually members one of another'. (Romans 12:05) A similar concept can be seen in the Bhagavad Gita which is an ancient text within Hinduism which reads: 'Although the Supersoul (God within), appears to be divided, He is never divided. He is situated as one.' (Bhagavad Gita 13:17) Mystical quotes within Islam come from Mohamed who recites: 'Man is my mystery and I am his mystery, for I am he himself and he is also I myself' (Shoghi, 1976) So I guess when you feel alone, you know that most religious scriptures tell you are not alone. We are all human and there will be other people in the world that get just how you feel, and do you know what there are some that have experienced it and now feel better! That tells you there is ability there for anyone to overcome their experiences. Even if you are not religious you still hold similarities to so many other people, we are all the same on a base level. Even scientists see that we are all the same on some levels.

Scientists have studied the makeup of who we are on a different level to religion, Albert Einstein released his most famous work in 1905, which suggested that mass and matter are different forms of the same thing. You may better recognise this equation as E=MC2, which in lay terms means that energy and physical objects are, on the smallest level, the same thing! (Einstein, 1905) This suggests that mass and energy are the same thing, so from this it seems we are the same... as light, as objects, as each other as everything!

If you imagine an Etch A Sketch toy from when you were a child: this toy allowed you to draw things that looked like objects and then shake it away. It was the amount of aluminium powder that came together to form the lines, but when shook it then separates in to nothing. Imagine that we are the condensed powder in the Etch A Sketch; other powder still exists around us, but it does not look solid because it isn't as condensed. Effectively we are all moving in a giant Etch A Sketch, only some things have more powder than other things. This idea is hard to get your head around, but this means that we are scientifically more connected than we maybe once thought. Think about this for a moment: you are part of something bigger than yourself. Up until now in the book we have looked at how we are alone in our experiences but using this concept shows that you are never alone; you share everything with everyone else. We are all in this together, there are bad people in the world that have hurt us, but there are good people in the world that can build us up. I hope that you feel a sense of shared feeling when you read this with the idea that other women who are reading this may have similar feelings to you. You are all reading this because you want to feel better about what someone else has imposed on you and wanting to feel better shows strength. This book may only be a stepping stone in your search for yourself, but this is your journey to search for the answers you need. The above paragraphs show my own journey in learning to accept abuse, but I do acknowledge that for many of you, you will need to walk your own paths. Search for answers where ever you can, because some where lies the things that you need to feel better. People can learn, grow and overcome everything if they try to make this happen. With the right mind frame, determination or the right support you can soon start to see that it is you that controls you. You do not have to be a victim; you still have a choice, and you can choose to change how you view your life.

There is beauty in the world that you can still access, despite what you have been through.

Chapter 9 looks at how we can find this beauty but first we look through Chapter 8 to find out who you are.

Chapter 8

Who are you, black sheep?

You call this a love bite?

Undoing Attachment Capture Syndrome

As mentioned previously women tend to be brain washed by their partner. It has been noted that their abuser would have been the biggest influence in their life. From your identity being captured you would now not be able to view yourself as independent and you may not even remember what ideas you had before your identity was changed.

People say, now you can get back to who you were before abuse, but for many women they don't even know who they were. This means it is even harder for women to find themselves because they have no reference of who they ever were before.

Picking apart your personality can be a good place to start getting to know who you really are. For any victim of abuse the need to get to know yourself is important and this journey is not easy. We look now at parts of identity that you can use to evaluate what fits you.

Who are you without your abuser?

It's OK to not feel like you did before; abuse does change you and will have changed you forever. But this does not have to be a bad thing. I liken being abused to people training to go to war:

You are broken down to your bare bones, criticised, tested, stripped of your identity. Your weaknesses are magnified, and you are not an individual anymore.

There is no doubt that you have been through an experience that has left you worse off than you were. Following this, you have opportunities to rebuild yourself in to the person that you always wanted to be. You can start by asking yourself, 'Who am I?

This seems like a broad question so let's break this down into small things that you can acknowledge to get to know yourself. People look to others for answers, but you have the answers; you just need to know 'you' better before you can heal yourself. So, who exactly are you?

Are you more extravert?

An extravert is a person who likes socialising and would rather attend a social gathering than stay at home. This type of person feels comfortable in social situations and needs human interactions to feel happy. If you were once an extravert but are now unsocial due to the experiences of your abuse, question whether you are happy being more unsocial. If no is the answer, then a personal goal could be to spend more time with others. If you are naturally an extravert, you may feel very low from being unsocial. Even if this is unachievable right now, this is an important part of getting to know you, so that you can easier recognise what you need to change to feel happier.

Are you more introvert?

An introvert is someone who prefers their own time, maybe in more quiet environments and does not like to be the centre of attention. If you are happy being on your own and can easily fill your time with things you want to do, then being an introvert is not an issue. This is who you are, and you may know that you are happier being in quieter places. If you are introverted due to issues that you have developed from your abuse, it may take time to become a little more extraverted.

Intuition

Being intuitive is a powerful tool that I feel often comes with being emotionally intelligent. As humans we are all intuitive to some degree: if we walk into our house, even if it's quiet, we can still feel the presence of life in that house if someone is there. This is not hocus pocus; this is how we have always been attuned to the world. We pick up on unspoken vibes of our world and we have done this way before language was invented.

The trouble with being an intuitive person is that you can sometimes get it wrong. Intuition teaches you to go with your gut feeling but following an abusive relationship your gut feeling could always be negative. You may connect negative feelings to everything due to your experiences of abuse. Intuitive people do sometimes get it wrong and judge situations on what they feel they know. Think about whether you react to quickly to your emotions, have they sometimes been wrong? After being in an abusive relationship it is important to use your rational mind as well as intuition.

Living with logic

Logical people tend to rarely act on emotions and will see the bigger picture of events that could occur. Clients often talk about the two voices that we hear in our heads, which are almost like the evil and good in us. Logical people can easily use their good voice to talk themselves out of feelings, events, situations and bad choices or temptations. Logical thinking allows you to work out the effects of your actions and allow you to make better decisions. You can not predict some things, no matter how much you logically think about them, but if you are logical you know when a situation is not going to end well for you. Being logical is only negative if it's destructive or negative for you. It is good to recognise the effects that your choices may have before you choose to make decisions.

Resilience

Sometimes in life we are met with mayhem, a situation that happens like getting into an abusive relationship. People cope with this type of mayhem in different ways. Some people see their experiences as progression and growth as a person, they may learn from the mistakes that they made. Others choose to hold on to the negatives and do not see their part in their experience; they feel that they had no choices.

I have heard many stories in the media of people who have had life-changing accidents that have changed the way they live. They have had to learn how to live again and accomplish a new style of living that suits their disabilities. Can we follow suit and do this with our emotions too? Can we learn to cope differently with stress and upset? This is not impossible; it is you that has this control over you, and you alone. Resilience is being able to feel negative emotions and still cope with them. Resilience is recognising things for what they are and accepting this. Everything is as it is in this life, but how we look at it makes it so. This notion is explained in the example below:

An ice cream shop has just run out of ice cream on a hot day. Jane visits the ice cream shop and is unable to get her ice cream. She walks away thinking, 'Ah well, I'll be able to have one tomorrow or next week, I might even stop somewhere else today.' Jane goes about the rest of her day and is happy.

Ben also visits the shop and is unable to get his ice cream. Ben goes away thinking, 'This always happens to me. I bet everyone else has had an ice cream today. It's just not fair, the day is ruined.'

Jane is more resilient here and can recognise that things happen sometimes, but there is always a next time. Ben struggles with resilience on this day and instead lets one bad event ruin his mind-set for the whole day.

Being resilient is looking at the bigger picture and realising that things sometimes just happen. How you deal with these things can impact your general wellbeing. For Jane she may have felt happy for the rest of the day, but this event ruined Bens whole day. For people who are not resilient they may find it difficult to let go of bad situations that happen. The act of storing all the bad events that happen in your conscious mind makes it seem like bad things always happen. The truth is that good and bad things happen all day every day. Ben may have walked past a man smiling, got free parking and had an amazing takeaway that evening. But Ben may have not acknowledged any of these nice things because he only holds onto the negatives that happen.

We all get days like this but on the days that we feel strong we should try and let go of negative emotions and realize that things can always become better. While we are still breathing, we have chances for things to be better. You have already been through an abusive relationship, and this shows that you have more strength than you probably give yourself credit for.

It is easier to be resilient when you stop asking, 'Why me?' The events that happen are what they are; it is only your mind that decides how you feel about it. Resilience is feeling upset, acknowledging it happened, rationalising it and then moving on. Some women say that some days they lack the motivation to be positive, because, changing negative thoughts is not easy! Here we look at motivation.

Motivation

Can motivation be learned? When we see Brenda at the gym and she is squatting a 40kg bar with her perfect peaches we can think, I wish I had that. But Brenda didn't get there overnight; maybe she has squatted for three years to get where she is. At the start of her journey she might not have had any motivation at all. The cruel thing about motivation is that you need to make a start before you feel motivated, but you can not start because you are not motivated. We want things immediately and we do not see the starting line because it is so far from the goal. Motivation is hard to get in the first place and the worst thing is, if we don't see any results quick enough, we will lose enthusiasm and stop. Motivation is hard to maintain when the goal seams unachievable.

Failures are inevitable when you are trying to achieve anything worthwhile. Motivation is what stops you from giving up, even when you fail, fall or lose. You need to put in serious effort to work towards something you want. This doesn't have to be perfect peaches or a career; it can be learning a new skill, getting fit or painting the house or even getting out of bed in the morning. If you lack motivation, start with something small yet challenging, stick at something, stick at anything. There is no better ingredient to grow motivation than to feel achievement for something that you set out to do. And remember to be kind to yourself, don't punish yourself when you fail, we all fail. Try to be motivated to try again.

Kindness

What is it to be kind? We could answer this question with so many different meanings: Don't knowingly cause harm, share, be selfless or always think of others. Being kind is all these things and many other things which show we care about others. The word selfish is usually looked at as a negative and to be called selfish is usually seen as an insult. But there is no word other than selfish that would describe being kind to yourself. So why is it that we look at being selfish as unkind when we sometimes should put our own feelings first. It is OK to think about yourself, you are you, so you must come first. Being kind should always start with being kind to yourself, do things for others but do not make that at the cost of your own feelings. We are taught to care for others, be empathic for others, but sometimes that overrides our own selves. To be kind to others will make you feel better, but you must keep some back for your own reserves.

I have unfortunately seen that the most giving people are taken advantage of. This is a cruel find in life, because it means that the kindest of people are taken for granted yet continue to give. Being kind does not always mean you are always willing and dependable. You can still be a kind person if you sometimes put your own feelings first. This is the difference between being kind and being completely selfless. Be kind, but do not always be selfless, keep some back for you. You can say no to people and it does not have to be confrontational, you can still be viewed by others as kind but also be assertive.

Assertiveness

Being assertive is a balance, you can stand up for yourself as well as be understood by others. Assertiveness is not easy if you have never spoken up for yourself. You might feel that being assertive is being argumentative, but this is not the case. Following an abusive relationship, you may feel that voicing your opinions will always cause conflict. You may want to avoid conflict at all costs and therefore choose not to voice your opinions. It is OK to voice your opinions; people can be reasonable if you are also reasonable. If you continuously choose not to voice your needs and opinions, you become a 'yeah, OK sure' type of person. This type of person says OK to everything they are asked even if they want to say no. You can only do this for a certain amount of time before you start to feel unappreciated.

Prolonged feelings of being unappreciated can cause aggression or the need to disengage completely with people. You might feel used and unconnected with others, which can make you feel like a victim of others. However, you are the other piece to this puzzle, conversations and agreements do not only have one person. They are two sided, you have your side and you can choose to say what you want. Saying no is not being nasty, saying that you don't agree is not being nasty. You can say no and then give your reasons, and you can also disagree and then give your reasons. This does not have to be a conflict, usually the other person will meet you with an 'OK' or choose to challenge you. Either way you are in a conversation and have a part to play in that decision. If you are stuck in the 'yeah, OK sure' position you could even voice that you feel you are always asked to do things. If you state your opinion that has a valid reason, you are being assertive not confrontational. You have the right to voice your feelings, and your feelings are just as important as anyone else's.

Optimistic

It is so hard to be optimistic if, so far, life has been difficult, you begin to expect bad things to happen. No one is predisposed to always having negative experiences, there is always the opportunity that things will be positive. Being optimistic is to be hopeful about the future, which might seem impossible to do at present. People say things like 'that's just my luck', when they feel unhopeful about their future. This is almost a self-fulfilling prophecy where you are so expectant of something going wrong that you sabotage it to go wrong. An example being:

A supervision session for work is coming up. You know that you have done a good job, but you go in to the supervisor and concentrate on the things you are doing wrong in the job. She gives you a slip of paper with all the bad things you told her you are doing in the job. You walk out thinking, 'Just my luck'. Even though you made this happen.

Admittedly not everything is as straightforward as this; sometimes things happen that you have no control over. But there is always a 50/50 chance that things can be good in the future. At times when it feels that things just continue to go wrong it is even more important to look at what is going right. To be appreciative of what is good in life can help you to feel more optimistic about life in general. I have seen children from third world countries play with a ball made from rags, all of them laughing as if they have no cares. I know how clichéd it is to encourage you to think that other people are far worse than yourself. But that is exactly what I have just done, because some people are optimistic that a ball of rags will make a football. Being optimistic comes with having gratitude of what you already have, to be positive about. Admittingly this is no where near easy, but some day's will be easier than others.

Self-awareness

Being aware of your own self is the best tool you can learn. When you know your needs, mechanisms, reactions, strengths and weaknesses you can be more stable. When you are self-aware you understand how your mind works and what you are and what you are not. As we have previously covered, when you are aware you can easily look at criticism from others and say, 'Yes, I think I agree with you', and then look at whether this is something you want to change. Or you can look at the criticism from others and say, 'No, I don't think I agree with that, I know you are being unfair in this judgment'. If you are self-aware you can use other's opinions of you to judge if they fit. To become self-aware is hard, because you must explore parts of yourself that you might not like, your faults, your daemons, your negative traits. No one is perfect but if we can honour ourselves the ability to be self-aware, we are less likely to live in sadness. Knowing what you need to make yourself feel better is the antidote to living well. We do not live in a world where we can easily see how to make ourselves feel better. Being self-aware enables you to understand what you need to do to feel happier because you begin to notice the real reasons why you feel sad.

We want faster cars, higher paid jobs, the latest phone, prettier faces and to be loved by all. But this is a superficial way to live, these things should not matter, we live in a world where things like this define our worth. Always thinking about how others view you is a self-indulgent way to live. Why does it matter how others view you if their ideas are based on unreal representations of you? This is not even you; this is the fake idea of you. Feeling fake by default makes you feel worse about who you really are. If you are truly happy with who you are you will care less about what others think of you. Separating yourself from how others see you is hard, because we often judge ourselves by what others think about us.

When you investigate who you are and find things you like about yourself based on your own personality you will be happier. You do not need confirmation from others that you are doing well. We are not in competition; we are in life and we all have different goals. Too many people live their lives through what they think others want. It is OK to just be you; the right people will make you feel happy to just be you.

Integrity

Integrity is having good morals and doing the right thing despite who will witness your actions. Having good morals is not giving a homeless man money then asking for a selfie to post what you did online. Integrity is:

- Being respectful of others
- Being honest with others
- Being sincere
- Not belittling others
- Not being rude to others

It would be ludicrous for me to say that you can hold integrity all the time. We are all only human, but we can make certain changes to the way we are. Integrity is choosing your actions based on the values you hold rather than based on what you can personally gain. When I was single and dating, I always used to watch the way my date spoke to the waiters. If someone is rude to others that are in a lesser position, this is not someone who has integrity. This is someone that would belittle others for personal gain, ironically this to them made them look powerful but it is in fact weak. The act of belittling the waiter intended to impress me with the power he had over another person, but infact this only showed me his weakness. In this scenario I apologised to the waiter and ended the date early, my date pleaded for me to forgive him. I explained that there was nothing to forgive for it was not me he belittled, he looked so confused by this that it made me question what forgiveness really meant.

Forgiveness

When you say 'I forgive you' what does that even mean? I understand why you did it? I'm OK with the fact that you did this? I accept that you did this? I think I know now that to give forgiveness means that you must let go of the hurt that someone caused. But what if they keep making the same mistake? Should you really give someone forgiveness if they keep inflicting harm in the same way. The idea of forgiveness can be very liberating and, in some contexts, to forgive may set you free of pain that others caused.

If you hold on to things that others did to you, this continues to hurt only you. Forgive someone for their actions but do not accept that the reasons given can excuse the same future actions. Forgive more than once if it serves you well but do not be senseless with acceptance. I don't think that 'I forgive you' means 'we can move forward together'; I think it means I can let go of what you did. Do not let your understanding of their reasons excuse continuous ill treatment, these reasons then, just become excuses. And saying I forgive you just becomes I accept what you continue to do. We must maintain our boundaries if we do not like people to act in certain ways.

We may choose to lower our boundaries if people possess the traits that we look for, but should we really do this?

What are your boundaries

Boundaries should be present in every type of relationship. We should have personal boundaries that we are aware of before we enter in to any intimate relationship. Everyone has different boundaries which they are comfortable with, but what would be considered healthy boundaries? We look now at brief examples:

- Saying no is your right

- It is not my responsibility to fix others

- It is not my responsibility to make others happy

- It is not my responsibility to meet the unfair needs of others

- I should not have to anticipate the desires of others

- My happiness is no one else's responsibility

- I know my own limits

- I must only do what I am comfortable to do

- I have a right to my own feelings

- I am worthy of commitment

- I deserve loyalty

- I should give loyalty

This chapter has looked at who we may be partly as a person, we now look at external things that can help to build our identity.

Chapter 9

Soul search for your identity

Funny how no one ever mentions those brown unicorns

Being you is OK

There is courage in being brave enough to be you – some people never feel enough but there is so much courage in being who you are. How wonderful it is to see someone confident enough in their own skin to show the colours that they wear on the inside. Do you know what colours you have on the inside? What are your likes and dislikes? What do you believe in? What are your passions?

Keep it simple

We looked at the power of language earlier in the book, and now, here, we revisit the idea of how we use language. We can use language to punish ourselves, we think about all the possibilities that we might fail in the future, in words that spiral in our head. We tell ourselves we are broken and continuously put words on how we feel emotionally: 'I feel sad; I am depressed; I am paranoid; I am anxious'. If we imagine a time before linguistics, we may have felt sad, maybe we would even look sad, but it wouldn't be voiced. Would this have meant that we could have searched for our own answers? We may not have looked for help from others because we would not have been able to ask for help.

If we imagine a simpler brain, much like animals of the world we see the body controls the brain and the brain makes the actions happen. A tiger that is hungry will have a pain of the stomach; they will feel hunger and then decide to hunt for food. There is no ability to express to someone that they are hungry, no ability to ask for food. Although this seems a far-removed analogy, we too have the power to create actions that can fulfil our needs. We have the answers to our own happiness; we just need to be more in touch with our needs. Doing rather than overthinking can be better for us, maybe we should take inspiration from the simpler brain of animals. If we have a clear goal in life and can engage in something that is meaningful, we would have little time to sit in our upset. I say this in the warmest possible way. Sadness is a symptom that is brought on by domestic abuse, but you do not have to live in this sadness forever, there is more life for you to live. Being abused takes your confidence in your ability to make decisions, but it does not take your worldly right to make them! You still have choices and you can choose to work towards feeling better.

You might be reading this and feel like you do not have the power to make choices and that you have no control over your future. This is OK; small steps to feeling better is where we start ... Rome was not built in a day. I have worked with many women who tell me that they are trapped in their lives and can not take any happiness from any part of how they live. I often encourage people to start small, what are the small things in life that you can take pleasure from?

If you look at success you will not have to look far to find the failed attempts. Failures are the stepping stones to becoming successful, and these can be used as the building blocks of knowledge. Before we begin to make goals, we must recognise what is important to us? What do we want to be successful in? Is it a personal achievement like to be able to do a handstand? Run a mile? Bake a cake from scratch? You might think that these tasks are small, but it is the mini successes that grow our confidence enough to conquer the big.

If you have no sense of identity, trying new things will help you to decide who you are. It will also help with your ability to make choices about what you do and do not want in your life. Trust yourself in what you like, get to know yourself and become who you want to be. Through this chapter we explore various elements in the world that can shape your identity as well as your experiences of the world.

Below is a list of things that we can do to explore who we really are as a person:

Do use music

When looking at the subject of music, you may think of a song, a band, festivals, singing or playing instruments. Music is everywhere in many forms and genres; apparently the universe plays its very own tune. Apparently if there were no other sounds on earth, we would only be able to hear the faint humming sound the universe makes when it is vibrating. This sound is a drawn out 'auuummm' sound and we can rarely here it due to overwhelming outside noises. If any of you have ever attempted to use recording equipment you will know that duplicating a sound makes it stronger. I use this idea to understand that in many people's opinions, saying the word Aum connects you to the vibrational sounds of the universe. Try saying the word Aum as slow and drawn out as you can, you should be able to feel vibrations resonating through your body. In this moment you are making the same sound as the universe; I think there is something cool about that but as noted earlier, I am weird.

Man-made music is an amazing tool. It is creative to personally make music, but it is also enjoyable to hear as an observer. Following the end of an abusive relationship, you may find that you are drawn to songs that are quite depressing. Weirdly many women say that they go through a period of listening to sad songs on purpose so that they can feel even more sad. On reflection of this process it is evident that many women don't feel like they can be sad after the end of their relationship. We have covered reasons for this such as the expectancy that they should be happy they are 'free' and 'safe'. Songs can make you feel sad, they can take you back in time, but they can also take you forward. If you can use music to bring out emotions, I propose that you could explore songs that are uplifting or encouraging when you feel ready. This could be songs about survival, songs that make you feel strong and new genres of music that are happier sounding than the usual depressive ones you listen to. Try avoiding music that reminds you of your darker days and explore new music that makes you feel good.

Do explore Writing

Writing isn't for everyone, but it is a creative way to express how you feel. This could be writing poetry, your own songs, stories a letter or just writing goals and plans for you future. Writing helps you to put your feelings on paper, which is a symbolic release. Reading what you have written can help you to process what you have been through. We are doing people, so when we experience things, we just do them, we do not always process what has happened. Writing about an event and re-reading what you have written somehow gives you the opportunity to read from someone else's eyes. It is easy to feel sorrow for others, but this can be more difficult to feel for yourself. When you re-read what you have written about your own experiences, it is almost as if they did not happen to you; in those moments' some women have said they felt sorrow for themselves that they have never felt before. This style of expressing yourself can be useful if you struggle with processing what has happened to you. Writing what has happened and how you feel gives us the wonderful ability to feel for ourselves. You might find that reading back your words is distressing because you are looking at them differently. If this happens, sit with the feelings and let them be processed; it is OK to feel sadness for yourself.

Writing can be used to help you to feel sorry for your own self, but it can be used in the opposite way too. If you feel sadness most of the time, then writing can be used as an escapism. Writing stories, or poetry that isn't connected to your abuse, can help to give your brain a rest from negative feelings. The act of writing can give focus to something other than the world and life you are living. Writing can almost be like taking a break from the stresses and upsets of everyday life.

<u>Do read</u>

Reading fiction helps you to focus on something intense that is not connected to your real life. In these moments you can be invested in other people's lives, thoughts, findings and stories. As adults most of us do not allow ourselves to get lost in story books like we did as children, but we should. The feelings that reading can evoke are real, reading other people's stories can allow you to feel certain emotions that you might not have felt for a long time. This process can help you to be more in touch with your own feelings about your life. Reading can also help you to explore what you like and what you do not like. There are so many books on so many different topics that there is sure to be a book that is suited to you. Books can give you some insight in to things that you may not have done in real life but exploring activities by the ink on paper can help you to decide what you like and dislike in the world.

Reading can also be used to help you to relax; it gives your mind a quietness from the anxieties you feel. There is a book for anything you are interested in; they can be used for escapism or learning. Learning something new can help you to feel a sense of achievement and more confident in yourself. Knowledge is power. There are many forums online and local book clubs in most library's that offer a place to go with your ideas. This may be the perfect opportunity to express your thoughts where others will listen, which can help you to feel valid.

Do Art

Everyone can try art, whether you are good at it or not you can create something from nothing. There are so many artistic things that you could try in your own home or in local events or lessons. There are so many different types of art. The most common are listed below:

- Painting
- Sketching/chalks/drawings
- Pottery
- Sculpture making
- Photography
- Jewellery making

Painting and drawing can allow you to express yourself in so many ways. All art is a therapeutic process, which forces you to be in the now, in this moment people have said they are usually calm and focused. Being in this state can help to dissolve anxieties and gives your brain a rest from what is going on in your life. You don't have to be an amazing artist to do art; just doodling or scribbling can be enough to make you feel more at ease.

Do Cook

Cooking is not just for the sake of eating; this can be used as an expressive task. Making food can give you self-worth because creating tasty food is a skill! Knowing what food's, you like and how to make them can help to build parts of your identity. Food is also nourishing and when you cook healthy food for yourself you are nourishing your body back to health from the inside out.

The saying 'you are what you eat' is well known, but I recognise that you also need a routine, if you do not have a set meal time it can make you feel depressed. Your body needs consistent good food so that your energy levels don't spike up and down. Eating sugary or high carb foods alone will make you feel more fatigued and down, it will also discourage you from eating healthy. You could take the time to learn how each type of food affects your body, treat yourself like a project: what food is good for what part of your mind/body? What do you need to feel better?

OK, so I have told you that food needs to be healthy, but what about baking as a hobby? Baking for others is fulfilling. Knowing how to bake is difficult and not everyone can do it. Some people are talented at this, and if you are lucky enough to be one of these people, know that this is a skill that not all possess and pat yourself on the back for this one!

Do sports

There are so many different sports, and as noted earlier in the book, exercise releases feel-good chemicals. Attending the local gym can be expensive and time-consuming but in today's world we don't have to. We can easily access videos online of at-home workouts; this can be with kettle bells, dumb-bells or body resistance exercises.

Having a structure to exercise can really help to motivate you back in to living life. You might even enjoy it. Activities that you could try if you are feeling adventurous are:

- Biking

- Running/jogging

- Swimming

- Entering races for charity

- Weight lifting

- Fitness classes

- Climbing

- Horse riding

- Cliff jumping

- Diving

- Coasteering

- Zip wiring

- Shooting

- Archery

- Skipping

- Pole fitness

- Trampolining

- Ice skating

- Tennis

- Surfing

If you are some one that is not able to engage in heavy activity, walking is just as good as any of the above sports. Walking outdoors in general can have a positive impact on your wellbeing. If you look around even the cleanest homes, you will find dust or the residues of cleaning chemicals. If we are in this home for long periods of time, we are effectively breathing in these things. Being outdoors gives your lungs and body the blast of clean oxygen that it needs to work at its best. Being in less populated places with more greenery can be the best medicine for your body. The levels of oxygen in forests or wooded areas are much cleaner. A walk outside can refresh your body; the clean oxygen flushes out all the stale indoor oxygen that you have been breathing. (David J Nowak, et al, 2014) Infact Richard Ryan a researcher and professor of psychology at Rochester University found that being out in nature increases positive wellbeing. He also reports that 90% of people have decreased exhaustion after being out in nature. (Ryan, R 2009) I see this as nature being a shot of espresso, but far cheaper!

Other studies have found that negative ions that are found in the air help to increase mood and cognitive ability. These ions are mostly found in places where there is crashing water and are proven to make you happier. Not only does being by the sea allow you to grab extra feel good ions, but other studies suggest that other things about the sea are of benefit to us. A study observed the brain activity of a large amount of people while staring at the ocean and it was found that their brain wave frequency was put in to a mile meditative state. (Terman, M, 1995) So science says; if you need a pick-me-up that is free, you know where to go.

Do Yoga

The idea of Yoga has unfortunately been hijacked by women who wear head bands and spandex which may have caused others to think it's fairly lame. While stretches and exercises are for sure part of yoga, this is not what yoga is all together. Yoga is made up of different elements. Yoga is also meditation, where you still the mind of things that distract your consciousness. Being aware of your consciousness is being aware of things that disrupt you from being at peace with yourself. (P., Yogananda, 1946) So, these things can be reaction emotions, insecurities, learned patterns of needs and living to please others. The art of yoga is being aware of these things so that you know who you really are without all the outside influences.

Yoga is also the stretches that are done in a composed way to connect your body and mind. Doing the physical side of yoga increases flexibility, self-confidence, strength, balance, awareness of your bodily feelings and stamina. (P., Yogananda, 1946) It also reduces pain, stress and can help you to have a better sleep pattern. Yoga helps you to be aware of your breathing; in fact, part of yoga is also breathing techniques alone. There has been much research which shows that breathing techniques help improve wellbeing. (Zeidan et al, 2013) There are many breathing techniques that are becoming more and more recognised as a form of treatment for some mental health issues. Many schools are now implementing aspects of yoga to children as the education system also recognises the benefits that this practice can bring. Two breathing techniques are below:

1: Sit cross-legged with your eyes closed, palms facing upwards and your head tilted upwards. Take a deep breath in, and on the out breath make a humming sound like a bee. This is the sound I mentioned earlier: Aum.

2. Sit cross-legged with your eyes closed, palms facing upwards and your head tilted upwards. Take a deep breath in breath out quickly while pulling your belly towards your spine. Repeat this up to 20 times. (Note: if you have a heart condition or breathing issues you should not attempt this exercise.)

Breathing in this way allows for better blood flow in to your body and can even allow more oxygen to reach your brain. More oxygen in your brain can help you to think and function better. (Zeidan et al, 2013)

Regulation of your breathing can also help to calm anxiety attacks. When you begin to have a panic attack your breathing gets faster and you may start to panic even more because of this. It's a circle situation where your breathing gets faster; you panic about your breathing, which then makes you breathe even quicker. By slowing your breathing down, you can stop yourself from having a panic attack. This idea has been around for a very long time, you may recall that you have seen a brown paper bag that is given to people to breathe in when they are panicking.

Do volunteer work

Believe it or not, many people say that when they do good things for others, they feel better in themselves. Volunteering somewhere can show you that many people will be grateful for your help. Being appreciated may have become an alien concept following an abusive relationship. Volunteering will not only help you to recognise your value to others but if you do not currently work it can also slowly integrate you in to a working lifestyle. During some abusive relationships the structure of the day can sometimes be a blur. Volunteering can be a subtle way of creating structure to your life, which can also bring a sense of purpose and meaning to you as a person. Getting back into a work environment after an abusive relationship can be really testing. If you are in a place where you feel too anxious to work or are to unconfident, volunteering is a good place to start. This experience will show you that you can make a difference and that you are of worth to people.

Do get inspired by a role model

Let's face it: not all people have had a good role model through life. If you have never had someone you look up to in life it can be very hard to find a sense of direction. It's never too late to use someone as a role model, there are so many amazing people in the world. Luckily with the use of media we have access to all kinds of inspirational people. It's always good to look at people as inspiration, to look at them and know that things are achievable. Whatever you aspire to be there will be someone in the world who is already achieving this. There are spiritual teachers, bloggers, singers, actors, writers, chefs and so many other people that we can take advice from.

Do anything new

Do you remember the last time you did something new? As we grow older, we get used to the world and rarely try things that we have not done before. Do you remember when you learned to ride a bike? If you do you may also remember how hard it was to learn to balance, change gear and stop without going over the handle bars. Learning a new skill is difficult, sometimes too difficult to pursue. After many failed attempts, my son learned how to ride his bike, with the help of my partner, my Mother and my Father, he finally did it. I recall my son's words when he first cycled without stabilisers; it was a moment that filled him with confidence. Confidence not only to ride his bike, but confidence in himself as a human living in the world. His words were, 'Look at me, I'm riding, I'm really doing it, I feel like I can do anything!' This really is the same ultimate inward feeling you get when you master something new in life. The sense of achievement you feel when you learn something difficult fills you with will power and the strength to achieve more.

For so many clients I have noticed that learning any new skills fills them with enthusiasm to live life again. During an abusive relationship, women are often stuck in a regimented way of living that is decided by their abuser. If you imagine a push bike that has not been used for a while, you know that it has gone rusty and difficult to use. You may need some oil and TLC to get the bike running again. Your brain may have become a rusty bike while you were in an abusive relationship, because the abuse just engulfs everything and stops you in your tracks. New skills are to your brain, like oil to a bike, and it may take a while before this bike works like it once did, or even better than before!

Do use apps

There are so many calming and self-help apps that can be used on a smart phone. Some apps allow you to follow pages that you like where you can explore ideas for new hobbies. This can help you to connect with the world again and pick you up if you feel low. You can choose to follow things you like, maybe even from the list of things above that you would like to try. There are also funny quotes and memes that can be found by following different pages which clients have said this has helped them to laugh when they have felt low. Some apps allow you to make your own boards where you can collect things that you like and save them to your own documents. This is identity building where by the touch of a button you can decide what you like and who you are. The world is at your fingertips.

Ditch the bad stuff

When you leave an abusive relationship, it can be easy to do things that are destructive to yourself. This is because you have had someone in your life that was destructive for you, and in some weird way, you then become that person for you. You have become accustomed to hearing negatives about yourself, so you now just tell them to yourself. While there are so many things that we can do to make us feel good about ourselves, there are just as many to make us feel bad. We look now at ways you can help to keep on top of being good to yourself.

Don't use social media in the wrong way

Social media can be a great tool to help you feel connected, but it can also be extremely destructive if used in the wrong way. We have explored the idea that it is good to have a role model. However, if you follow role models that make you feel bad about yourself, this is destructive to you. Social media allows you to follow models/musicians/artists/millionaires, which can be inspiring. These people can be looked at as influential but if you find yourself comparing yourself to them rather than being inspired by them, this may be unhealthy for you.

Social media has not helped to make us feel happy about who we are. We have created a world that has allowed for even more unawareness in people. We show the best sides of ourselves; people are desperate for the perfect picture to show how amazing their life is. In Doing this I feel we are robbing ourselves of the chances to be happy by wanting to look happy to others. I watched a sunset not long ago and took a photo. Alongside me were three other people that were taking photos. Two walked away straight after they took the picture; they did not even stay to look at the sunset. Why? I imagined, like many other people I know they took the picture to show to others, but they didn't live it ... they didn't stare at the sunset ... they didn't take it in. We live in a world so lost in how others see us that we have lost the need to experience things for ourselves. Do we even follow what we like anymore? Or do we like what we think others would like us to like? You are free to make choices that will shape your future, you are free to become who you really are, you are free to grow, you are free to live the life you choose. Live for you and not for others, get to know what you like, and like that for you.

We live in a world that feeds off our insecurities and unfortunately after an abusive relationship we are so much more susceptible to this influence. Pages are made via social media for how to get whiter teeth, smaller waists, thinner thighs or better skin. We are continuously told by social media that we are not good enough, that we need to improve, we need to be different. We are targeted by adverts telling us what we need to be an adequate human being. We concentrate on the negatives so much more than any positives that we can lose sight of anything we like about ourselves. If you cannot take inspiration from others, then be your own role model. Celebrate the positives and do not concentrate on the negatives. Did you shower this morning? Yes? Tick! Well done you, that's great. Did you drink a huge glass of water this morning to keep your body hydrated? Yes? Tick! So that would be two ticks on the 'being good to yourself' life score. These may not seem like big achievements, but these are the small things that are going to make you feel better one small step at a time. Keep taking small steps and before you know it you will be a million miles away from where you were.

Social media can also be used to check up on people, and if you are someone who still feels attached to your ex-partner you may want to check up on them. Social media is so instant, things that have been impossible to see before are now attainable by just clicking buttons. It would be bizarre to drive to your ex-partner's house and walk in to his home to have a look at his new girlfriend. Yet social media allows you to do this: you can look in to your ex-partner's life. So many women I have worked with become obsessed with checking their ex partner's social media. Many say it's because they need to know if he has changed or that they just can't believe that he has moved on. Checking social media can be a self-sabotage; it is rarely going to make you feel better. It will more than likely make you feel worse as it is an easily accessible reminder that could be stopping you from moving on.

Don't have too many late nights

For some people it is impossible to get a good night's sleep. However, there are certain things that are becoming publicly promoted to help you to get a better night's sleep:

- Eating or drinking before bed can keep you awake because your body is now working to burn off what you have had. This can affect your sleep pattern as you are tired, but your body is awake.

- Caffeine can affect your sleep pattern. This affects everyone differently; some people are more susceptible to caffeine than others. Caffeine can keep you awake and cause you to feel anxious. If you are a big caffeine drinker and struggle with sleep, try and limit your caffeine to mornings and midday only. Caffeine may be hidden in drinks and foods so check the labels if you are unsure of what you are drinking/eating.

• Using a smart phone before bed can also effect being able to get to sleep and the quality of sleep, the light that is submitted from your phone tells your brain it's light outside. So, your rhythm of sleep pattern is out of sync with the time of day it is. There are different filters on your phone that can help with this such as the blue light filter, which is not as bright as your average screen. However, the brightness of a phone can still knock you out of sync.

• Thinking negative thoughts before bed can make you spiral into an anxious feeling where you can't stop thinking about things.

• A bedtime routine can help to relax you and your mind; this could be by having a bath, meditation or reading a book.

You are invited in to Chapter 10 to have a look at all the tasks that I have carried out in my counselling rooms. These tasks have helped many women to overcome the impacts of their abuse. Not all will be suited to you as overcoming abuse is an individual thing, however some should fit with what you need.

Chapter 10

Healing yourself slowly to forward

Thanks, past, for all of your lessons; and, no, you will not interfere

with my future plans

Where is the magic?

By this point in the book you might have an idea about what your vulnerabilities are. We have explored being childlike in negative ways, but what about ways that we can use this in a positive way? We sometimes maybe need to take a trip back to positive things from childhood that encouraged you to develop. We lose the wonderment that children experience through becoming complacent of the world around us. When have you ever seen an adult study the veins of a leaf like a child would? Why do we lose the magical views of the world around us as we grow older? There is magic in the world and I ask you to go back to basics with this. Domestic abuse can bury any wonderment that we have left as an adult but cruelly also brings out all the vulnerabilities of being a child. We are all victim of losing parts of ourselves as we grow, but what if we should have kept some of these parts? Regardless of age and your experience of abuse I encourage you to revisit your positive childhood attitudes, hobbies and quirkiness. This chapter now looks at different ideas of self-help tasks that have helped me as well as some of the women I have worked with, each heading throughout this chapter looks at a new concept.

Fairy tales

Children love to be told stories. I have never seen eyes so big as when a child is waiting for the next sentence of a story. It's magic for children, but our ideas of fairy tales have been ruined by the reality of the world. Princes do not exist; in fact, some men are the opposite. But what about if we can capture some of the feelings that we had as children. We can still be imaginative in our thinking as adults; this ability doesn't just disappear. We just find it difficult to let go and immerse into this because we have a million other things to think about, worry about and get stressed about.

Meditation is like stories in ways; it takes us away from the reality that we live. Meditation can help you to overcome the symptoms of abuse by changing the way you think and feel. Although we have previously looked at what meditation is, and the benefits let's look now at the science of it. Scientists have found that when meditation is practiced regularly, the neural pathways to limbic system are lengthened. This in simple terms means that the parts of your brain that are responsible for reasoning, creativity and emotions, grow! This means that you have more time to think about emotions before you react, so it will lessen your reaction emotions. It will make you more able to reason and understand others. (Zeidan et al, 2013)

Meditation has also been scientifically linked to reducing anxiety and social anxiety. Studies have shown that the act of daily meditation sessions over eight weeks has lasting effects and can reduce anxiety for years. (Zeidan et al, 2013) Doing meditation only a few times has been shown to improve concentration and attention. (Mrazek, 2013) So science says that meditation will make you feel calmer and more focused. My own understanding of this highlights to me that domestic abuse victims more than anyone need the benefits of mediation. The first part of this chapter looks at different styles of meditation. We explore the idea of being in the now to help focus the mind, just like the effects of meditation.

The idea behind the following exercises is that your brain is very much in control of your feelings.

Exercise 1

1. Sit with your legs crossed on the floor, or upright in a chair. Set your hands on your thighs with your palms facing upwards. Tilt your head slightly back and close your eyes.
2. Imagine that you are at the beach, any beach that you can find good memories of. You are standing by the sea edge.
3. Imagine there is a breeze in the air that feels so strong. You can feel it hitting your body. You can hear the howling noises in your ears.
4. Picture the waves: they are fierce and big; almost out of control. Are they mostly white? Blue? Green?
5. There are birds in the air that are flying to find shelter from what seems like the start of a storm.

6. The sun begins to peek out ever so slowly and the wind starts to drop. Imagine the sun on your skin. What does it feel like?

7. A bird is flying towards you, but it's not like any other bird. It is the most beautiful bird you have ever seen, and it has something in its mouth. It's a necklace.

8. The bird flies over you and drops the necklace into your hands. You look at the necklace and it has a symbol on it that is moving. It's a picture of a butterfly leaving a cocoon. The butterfly comes out of the necklace and turns in to a real butterfly.

9. You watch this butterfly until it flies so high you can no longer see it. At this point you can open your eyes.

Exercise 2

The following exercise invites you to use your visual imagination to let go of negative feelings and take in positives:

Step 1: Sit with your legs crossed, eyes closed, and head tilted slightly upwards. If you cannot sit on the floor sit upright in a chair.

Step 2: Imagine breathing out negative feelings, visually give them a shape, like a cloud, and a colour that you feel is negative. Imagine this as the breath leaves your nose/mouth.

Step 3: Imagine breathing in positivity and give this a different colour that you feel is positive. And a more positive form such as a light. Imagine this as you breathe in.

Step 4: Repeat this a few times, each time making the breath stretch further and longer so that the cloud you breathe out grows. And the breath you take in becomes a bigger and longer form of light.

Step 5: Imagine the earth opening, so far down you can see the earth's fire core. Imagine on your out breath the negative cloud reaches down right into the earth core.

Step 6: On your in breath imagine the positive light you are breathing in coming straight down from the sky above, bringing positivity into your body. Continue step 5 and 6 until you can feel a line flowing through you from the earth's core to the sky.

Step 7: when you are ready, close this mediation by imagining the earth swallowing your negative thoughts. Then imagine the positive light shooting down from the sky and entering your body.

We have looked at separating the mind and body throughout this book to understand that they are two different parts of you that do not always interact. The exercises above should help you to put a visual on feelings and therefore help your mind to let go of negativity you feel.

Next, we explore a different type of exercise where you are more in reality than story mode. This style of exercise can help you to feel more connected to the world around you.

Visuals in the real world

Going for a walk down a road, path or street that you have been down before can be boring. You have walked this route so many times that you are on autopilot, and maybe while walking you are thinking of what time it is, what to have for tea or what is on TV tonight. Again, as adults, we just do not see the magic in the world, because we are just used to it. We are complacent of the wonder in the world and rarely think of the complexities of it. A child thinks differently. I see this first-hand when I walk with my son and see that he is so engrossed in the world that he can't answer my question of, 'What do you want for tea?' Instead he says things like, 'Look at that slug. Where is he going?' We take the world for granted by living in our heads. We live in a fast-paced world, which means we are always thinking about the next thing we need to do.

Taking in the world around you gives you a rest from the stress of life. If you can find wonder in the small things in your life, you really will begin to appreciate life itself. We have senses that we take for granted, but if we become aware of using them, everything may start to feel good. Try taking in your surroundings and use all senses to do this. This could be done in any simple daily task you do. See some examples of this here:

1. **Washing your hair**: how do your fingers feel on your head? What does it smell like? How does the water feel? If you close your eyes do things feel different?
2. **Eating a meal**: how does the food smell? What colours are in it? How does the food feel in your mouth? What does each thing taste like? How does it feel when it is going down your throat? Does your stomach feel different?
3. **Walking**: what sounds can you hear? Can you see any animals? Are there any cracks in the pavements you didn't see before? Are there trees and leaves? What do the trees look like close up? What do they feel like to touch? What does the sky look like? What is the first object you can see that meets the end of the sky? What does the air smell like? What does the air feel like?
4. **Making tea**: What colour is the tea? How does it look when you stir it? What shape is the steam?

Using your senses helps to ground you in the world around you. With this style of exercise some clients report that they begin to feel calmer and more relaxed in their thinking.

Positive breathing

Regulating your breathing can really help to calm you down. People underestimate the power of breathing exercises, considering that they have been used for thousands of years.

Try the following exercise: you breathe in and out slowly while saying something on the in breath and something on your out breath. You can make your own choice of two sentences that are meaningful to you. Two examples of what you could say could be:

Example 1

Inhale: I am OK with who I am
Exhale: I am enough as I am

Example 2

Inhale: I am powerful
Exhale: I have control

During this exercise you might find that your thoughts drift away and you end up thinking of many other things. If this happens just pull your mind back to the words you are saying in your head. This is not an easy thing to do and it may take you numerous attempts before you can easily relax into doing this. I personally have used this style of breathing off and on for over six years. I now notice that if I feel anxious or negative through the day, I only need to repeat the words in my head once in order to feel better.

Positive affirmations

I feel that the best thing about learning about your weaknesses is that you come to realise that you have the power to change them! This is not an easy task and it will not happen overnight; it may take you time to believe in yourself. Negative thoughts that I have continuously heard from clients are: 'I am weak'; 'I feel unworthy';

'I feel used'. All these statements seem to point towards feelings of vulnerability. You can undo the negative effects in the reverse way that they were created by your abuser! You may have been told repeatedly that you were stupid, and now you believe that you are stupid. You can tell yourself repeatedly that you are clever, and you will eventually feel clever.

Choose a positive sentence about yourself and say this in the mirror three times every morning and night and see how you feel within the coming weeks. You could even say the words in your head throughout the day if you experience upsetting emotions. You could record in your diary how you feel from day to day about their effects. Words to describe yourself could be as simple as:

I am enough

This affirmation can be powerful to say to yourself: the acceptance of yourself as enough is an important part to feeling better. You might not believe your chosen affirmations at first, but over time just as you were brainwashed, you can un-brainwash yourself.

Nightmares are real

I have worked with so many women who say that they have nightmares that wake them up at night. On investigation their nightmares are always symbols that represent their life events and feelings. An example of an abuse victim's nightmare is seen below:

I was in a forest and all these monkeys were calling me to get up to the trees. They were screaming from the trees for me to try and climb up high with them. They kept saying, 'It's coming for you', and I didn't understand what they meant. Suddenly, a huge gush of sea water comes through the forest and whooshes me away. I can't breathe, and all the monkeys are screaming for me. I start to drown. As I look up at the trees through the water, one monkey says, 'It's ridiculous that she didn't climb up here.'

This nightmare may seem bizarre but what if I told you that the monkeys represented this woman's family. The fact she could not get up to them represented how trapped she felt in her abuse. The height of the trees represented the distance she felt between her and her family in their understanding of her abuse. The sea represented her ex-partner, and her death represented her identity. The comment from the monkey at the end highlighted how her family didn't understand why she did not leave her abuser. From looking in to client's dream's in my counselling room I have noticed that nightmares and dreams can help you to process what you really think about a situation. Next time you have a bizarre nightmare that doesn't make sense, try and work out the meaning.

Task

Can you pull on positive memories of a time where you were who you wanted to be? This can be a time where you felt strong and happy. This can be any time in your life where you remember feeling OK. Answer the questions here:

1. What was good about you at the time?

2.What mindset did you have?

3.What would have to change to achieve one or all these points?

4. Realistically how can you achieve these points again?

Tasks to help with the impacts of abuse

Many women find it difficult to cope with the impacts of domestic abuse. Victims often have no idea of ways that they can control their thoughts, they often feel powerless over the way they feel. Throughout my counselling career I have helped victims to carry out tasks that have allowed them to take control of their emotions and thoughts. Listed below are tasks and guidance that has worked to help victims overcome the impacts of abuse. We are all individuals, therefore not all tasks and guidance will suit you but there should be a few that you can use.

- Place a photo of your ex-partner outside your door and under an outdoor mat and proceed to use the mat as normal. Some women feel that this symbolises gaining control back from this person. Others like to imagine that as the picture becomes destroyed so does any connections to the abuse. Some clients have said that the act of closing the door behind them, shut him out.

- Placing memories in a box can be a good way of storing things that you do not want to think about. Some clients have used a memory box in their imagination and imagined putting their negative thoughts in the box. Other clients have used actual shoe boxes, placing thoughts that they have written on paper inside. They have then closed the lid on the box and visualised this to be closing the lid on the thoughts and feelings.

- Following experiences of domestic abuse some people find it difficult to express their emotions. Using real life analogies can help to bring out emotions that would be impossible to feel on your own. The world around us is full of settings that we can liken to our own feelings. The wind, rain and the sea can be chaos, beautiful, calm or aggressive depending on the conditions at the time. You can use these analogies sometimes to try and connect with your feelings. I have likened feelings to the crashing waves at sea on a windy horrible day. Watching the unruly sea has helped some clients to connect with feelings of being out of control. This can be done with the weather conditions or any part of the natural world that you can relate your feelings to. Just as the weather is aggressive and out of control, so too are our feelings, but, without doubt, calmness follows. No storms last forever.

- As we explored in earlier chapters, if you have experienced physical or sexual abuse you may have difficulty with skin contact. Many clients have said that they do not want to be touched as they feel negative emotions when receiving any form of contact. Visualisation is an amazing tool when working with this type of issue. Visually imagining the negatives that you feel as a colour, smoke, or liquid that is in your skin gives your feelings a form. With this you can then visualise the form leaving your skin and disappearing into the air so high that it has gone. If you are someone that cannot easily use imaginative imagery, you could use things around you to help you to do this. This could be while taking a bath or shower (not too hot) you imagine the steam or water leaving your skin is all the negative emotions and impurities that you feel.

• Writing negative thoughts or feelings down on paper and then burning them can symbolise them disappearing. Some clients have used their memory shoe box papers to do this. While watching them burn they have imagined all the thoughts drifting away with the smoke. (Obviously I don't need to tell you fire is dangerous, but I will anyway: be safe if you choose to do this. Check local council rules on having fires and check safe ways to have one)

• Burying things that remind you of your abuser can help you to symbolically dispose of them. Some had receipts from dates, cards, a picture or a gift that was given to them. The act of doing this might not suit everyone but for some the idea that they have buried them symbolises the death of the relationship. For these clients the burial site is important as they can choose to revisit it to remind themselves that he is gone.

- With intrusive thoughts about the past many clients attempt to try and stop thinking about them. This can show that they fear the memories and thoughts just as much as experiencing them. I experienced this issue myself and asked my own supervisor what I should do. She explained that the problem with pushing thoughts away is that you won't process them so they may never go. If you have an intrusive thought that is difficult to think about it may be important to acknowledge it rather than try and stop the thought. Sitting with the thought and watching is pass helped me to move on from it, and the day I did this was the last time that this thought entered my mind.

- If you experience thoughts that replay as if you are there going through it you can try to change your actions in the thought; rather than reliving what happened, change what happened in your thought. We look here at an example of what I mean by this. Let's say that you have a thought that you were being hurt by someone and you relive it as if you were there. Imagine something different happening in this memory, this can be anything that you can change about it from the surroundings to what was said. This can sometimes help you to see that you now have control over your thoughts.

- If you replay thoughts as if you are a third person you may see the thoughts that replay as a movie reel in your head. In this instance you can try and control things like the colour of the memory, change the colour of the whole scene or just parts of it. Imagine that the whole scene is in a bubble and float it away. The act of doing these things again makes you see you have control over these thoughts; the thought of them can become less feared.

- The power of breathing in and out slowly is underestimated. Breathing can help to regulate the way that your body is working. If you are panicking about something, you should try and reduce the speed of your breathing. This can fool your body into calming down. The trouble with a panic attack is that you feel physical symptoms like sweaty palms, shaking, heart palpitations, dry mouth and maybe sickness. All these bodily feelings make you feel like you have no control over this attack. When your body receives a calming flow of oxygen it sends the message to all your organs and brain that you are OK. The power your body must regulate itself is unbelievable, but you just need to give it some help.

- Practice meditations found in this book daily if you can, or as you feel you need them. As previously noted, you are likely to have long-term effects on controlling your emotions.

- As suggested previously use your senses, look for things you can see, things you can touch, things you can hear, things you can smell or things you can taste.

- Shake it out. Shaking your hands quickly can make you feel better. All built-up stress and energy that needs to come out can be shook off. If you feel angry this would work as you are expelling energy; if you feel sad this can help you to feel more alive. You could even use the visual technique and shake out negative feelings in different colours.

• Be appreciative of what is going right. Being appreciative can help to overcome negative feelings associated with abuse. When you wake up in the morning, say three things to yourself that you are happy for on this day. This could be anything from your sight, mobility, health, family, friends, warmth or home. There is so much to be grateful for, but we too easily see only negatives. Acknowledge the positives over the negatives and your mindset will start to become more positive by default.

• Treat yourself kindly, make time for yourself, treat yourself good. This can be to read, take a bath, or any of the activities mentioned in this book. Self-care comes first, you haven't been shown care through abuse, so you need to give this to yourself now. You cannot expect someone else to look after you, you must be this person for your own self. You are there to keep yourself safe and well; do not be unkind to yourself.

• Do not underestimate the power of helping others; if you have advice or can help someone, do it. Helping others can help to build self-worth; this can be by helping someone with something that you are good at that they are not. We all have strengths and weaknesses; you will be better at some things than others.

• Know your worth; remember that you are equal to others even if you feel like you are not. You are just as worthy as anyone else on the planet. You have been in an abusive relationship, which tells me you did not recognise that you were worth more than what you were given. Look at the ways that you are worthy and learn to appreciate yourself in who you are. We cannot enter a healthy relationship with others if we do not see our own worth.

• When you need connection and feel alone, smile at someone or be kind to them. Sometimes when we do these things, we feel appreciated and this shows us we have power in the world with others. Admittedly, to do this every day may be too selfless, so practice this when you feel like it naturally. It is surprising how happy it can make you to get a smile, a wave or a thank you from a stranger. People appreciate you and can show appreciation to what you offer them in the world.

- Take time to focus on one thing; trying to be amazing at everything just does not work. You will be everywhere and nowhere at the same time. Tackle things step by step, set one goal at a time and things will feel less hectic. There are many tasks throughout the book that you can revisit to look at goals you may have, the concept of one at a time is best when aiming to achieve.

- Check in with yourself more often, you need to listen to your feelings, are you tired? Sad? Angry? Why is this? Try to address your feelings as they happen and do not push them down. When we do this, we are more likely to experience the coke bottle situation. Everybody can have down days; feeling OK is not a place that we can stay 100% of the time.

- Remember that everything is as it is; it is the act of thinking that makes it so. By this, I mean that how you think about a situation makes it good or bad. If we believe nothing will get better, we will always look at situations negatively. Do not rob yourself of your positive thoughts, things can be good, nothing is always going to be bad.

- Carry out the task in this book to track your feelings, some clients that have completed this task have been able to recognise what makes them sad and why.

- Learn something new, this can be from the list given in the previous chapter. Why do this? Because learning something new fills your brain with new memory, as well as keeps your focus on the now. Old memories that are trauma based may never be completely forgotten, but learning new things makes the now ever more important than the past. You do not have to be who you were in your past, learning something new changes you as a person.

- Do not be too hard on yourself, many people will be too hard on you in life, do not be one of them! You might be to judgmental of yourself and your actions, this brings shame, guilt and feelings of low self-worth. Try and evaluate your situation and imagine that you are talking to a friend rather than yourself. What advice would you give a friend that feels like you do? Be your own friend, not your own bully.

- Know that rest and recovery must be part of moving forward. Taking a rest does not mean that you are taking a step backwards, it means that this is what you need to do now to keep moving forward. There are no steps back, mistakes that you make do not undo the distance you have already travelled.

- You cannot control everything, but after an abusive relationship you might want to control everything. The idea 'whatever will be' is a refreshing way to live, the future is out of your hands. The truth is you can micro manage and plan every detail of the future, but there will always be outside factors that might stop the plan. You cannot and will not control everything. Me and my best friend Kelly continuously tell each other 'what will be will be' because this can be so weight lifting and can help you to let that go.

It's OK to be a little mad

It's OK to feel a bit unstable at times, nothing in this life is continuously functioning, even machines break! Have the courage to be imperfect, because this is normal! It's OK to be a little insane if it doesn't affect you or others negatively, because all of us are a little insane in some ways! You do not need to feel in fear of people who look like they have it all together. You are just as able as anyone else on the planet, we are after all made up of the same things! The idea that OK is a state of being is just not rational, we all dip in and out of OK, because living is hard. Living can be even harder after you experience abuse. Every day you rise out of bed is an achievement, you are still here, still living, despite what you have been through. This makes you strong at the start of every single day!

Using the information and tasks in this book can help you to reach feeling OK. I hope that you can return to ideas in this book when you are not at OK, so that you can find your way back! When the chaos that fills life becomes too much, take it back to basics, because these things work. Self-help is exactly that, although I have given you ideas of how to feel better, how you use them is now down to you. No one can truly help you, as much as you can help you, you may not feel powerful now but, you are in control of you.

We have power in the world, we are all there is now, all there is to come, and all there ever was!

Find out what works to keep you mentally and physically safe and keep returning to these things. Find the moments in life that bring you happiness whatever they may be, and let me tell you, when you reach these moments, and I mean really reach there, you can be free.

I have shared with you my ideas of freedom...... now how you get there, is on your own.

References

Bhagavad-Gita, Chapter 13 *Nature, the Enjoyer, and Consciousness,* Verse 17.

BBC (2013) BBC Science, *What is stress,* Available at: http://www.bbc.co.uk/science/0/21685448

BBC (2014) BBC Science, *Human body and mind, Emotions and instincts, Science of love,* Available at: https://www.bbc.co.uk/science/hottopics/love

BBC (2019) Radio 4 in four, *Is narcissism on the rise?* Available at: https://www.bbc.co.uk/programmes/articles/sfHxNf7X4jpZ424Dwl6 Fjk/is-narcissism-on-the-rise

C., Sousa, T., Herrenkohl., C., Moylan, E., Tajima, J., Kika, M., Russo (2010) *Longitudinal study on the Effects of Child Abuse and Children's Exposure to Domestic Violence, Parent-Child Attachment, and Antisocial Behaviour in Adolescence.* Journal of interpersonal violence. Available at: https ://www.ncbi.nlm.nih.gov/pmc/articles/PMC2921555/

D., J., Nowak, S., Hirabayashi, A., Bodine, E., Greenfield, (2014) *Tree and forest effects on air quality and human health in the United States,* Elsevier Ltd, USA. Available at

https://www.fs.fed.us/nrs/pubs/jrnl/2014/nrs_2014_nowak_001.pdf

Einstein, A, 1905, *E=mc2*, American Journal of Undergraduate Research, Volume 13, Issue 1, January 2016

Fadel Zeidan, Katherine T. Martucci, Robert A. Kraft, John G. McHaffie, Robert C. Coghill; *Neural correlates of mindfulness meditation-related anxiety relief,* Social Cognitive and Affective Neuroscience, University Press, Volume 9, Issue 6, 1 June 2014, Pages 751–759, https://doi.org/10.1093/scan/nst041

Freud., S., (1905) *Fragments of analysis of a case of hysteria, Dora,* n The Freud Reader, P. Gay, (Ed). London: Vintage.

L., Provenzi, G., S., Di Minco, L., Giusti, E., Guida, M., Muller (2018) Disentagling the *Dyadic Dance: Theoretical, Methodological and Outcomes Systematic Review of Mother-Infant Dyadic Processes, Centre for the at-risk infant,* Frontiers in Psychology. Available   at:

https://www.ncbi.nlm.nih.gov/pmc/articles/PMC5868133/

Michael D. Mrazek, Michael S. Franklin, Dawa Tarchin Phillips, Benjamin Baird, and Jonathan W. Schooler, 2013 *Mindfulness Training Improves Working Memory Capacity and GRE Performance While Reducing Mind Wandering*, Volume: 24 issue: 5, page(s): 776-781, Sage journals, available at:

https://journals.sagepub.com/doi/abs/10.1177/0956797612459659

Office for National Statistics *(2016) Focus on Violent Crime and Sexual Offences,* 2014/15 Available at:

https://www.ons.gov.uk/peoplepopulationandcommunity/crimeandjustice/bulletins/domesticabuseinenglandandwales/yearendingmarch2018

P., Yogananda, (1946) *Autobiography of a Yogi*, The philosophical library, India and United Stated

R., M., Ryan, N., Weinstein, J., Bernstein, K., W., Brown, L., Mistretta, M., Gagne, (2010) *Vitalizing effects of being outdoors in nature,* Elsevier, USA. Available at:

https://www.sciencedirect.com/science/article/abs/pii/S027249440900838#!

Romans, 12:05, *Holy Bible*, English standard version

Shoghi Effendi, 1976, *Gleanings from the writings of Baha' U' Llah*, Bahai

S., Sweetnam (2013) *Where do you think domestic abuse hurts most?* Sage journals, University of Toronto, Ontario, Canada Available at:

https://journals.sagepub.com/doi/abs/10.1177/1077801212475340?journalCode=vawa

Terman., M, Terman., J.S, (1995) *Treatment of seasonal effective disorder with a high-output negative ionizer*, Department of psychiatry, Columbia University, New York City, USA. Available at: https://www.ncbi.nlm.nih.gov/pubmed/9395604

T., Mcadams, F., V., Rijsdijk, J., Narustye, J., M., Ganbian., D., Reiss, E., Spotts, J., M., Neiderhiser, P., Lichtenstein, T., C., Eley (2016) *Associations between the parent–child relationship and adolescent self-worth: a genetically informed study of twin parents and their adolescent children,* Journal of Child Psychology and

Psychiatry and Allied Disciplined. Available at:

https://www.ncbi.nlm.nih.gov/pmc/articles/PMC5215430/

Tracey Jenkins & Jennifer Dunne Equal Opportunities Commission

August (2007) Equal Opportunities Commission: *Domestic Abuse,*

The Facts: A Secondary Research Report. Available at:

http://www.assembly.wales/NAfW%20Documents/cc_3__da10_-

_ehrc.pdf%20-%2023082010/cc_3__da10_-_ehrc-English.pdf

[Accessed on 05/03/18

As cited from http://www.refuge.org.uk/get-help-now/what-is-domestic-violence/domestic-violence-the-facts/

W., Shakespeare, (1914) *Hamlet, Prince of Denmark,* Act III, Scene

II

W., Shakespeare, (1623) *As you like it,* Act II Scene VII

Acknowledgements

Thank you to all my family and Kelly for being OK with all the cups of coffee I missed with them while I carried out this work. Thank you to my husband who continuously believes in me and is now by my side for the rest of journey. I would also like to thank Christine Brown and Parvin Boyle for helping me through the darkest days of my abuse; without you I might not even be alive. Thank you from the bottom of my heart to my favourite artists Herakut for giving me the copyright to use their unbelievable art work. And the biggest thank you goes to my son, for making me want to be a stronger version of myself.

Then it was time to let go.

Contacts that can help

The live fear free helpline is a 24-hour helpline in England and Wales that can provide advice around domestic abuse. They can help with refuge spaces for people who are looking to be immediately safe as well as many other types of help. (08088010800)

Women's aid has many places across England and Wales, where you can gain access to support or advice in any areas of your abuse. The national number is (0808 2000247)

You can call 101 if you want to report a crime from England, Wales, Scotland and Northern island. This is a non-emergency number where you can ask the police for advice.

The stalking helpline can give you advice on some one that may be stalking you. The national number is (08088020300)

Download the Hollie Guard app from your smart phone for additional safety where needed. This enables you to appoint a safe contact that will be contacted to alert them of your safety.

You can call 999 in any situation where you feel you are at risk of harm.

Printed in Great Britain
by Amazon